city of the Palio

Text by:
MARCO BORELLA

DISTRIBUTORE ESCLUSIVO PER LA TOSCANA
Mag.: 50019 OSMANNORO - SESTO F.NO (FI)
Via Tevere, 102 Int. 6
Tel. (055) 301212 - Telefax (055) 301239

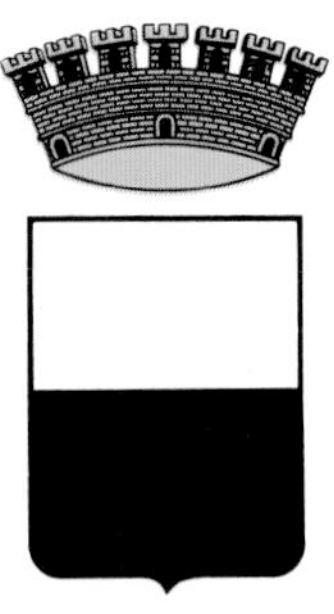

INTRODUCTION

Placed in the central position of the Tuscany highlands, between the catchment basins of Arbia and Elsa, Siena reveals itself to the traveller on three steep hills, separated by equally steep valleys. The brickwork town buildings and above all the steep, close, multilayered roofs, gathered together in a reddish-brown mass, the hard profile of the town created by the body of its outstanding monuments, anticipate the evocative atmosphere of a noble medieval town, enclosed by walls and firmly placed on the hills, which has well preserved the original urban plan. It is remarkable to be able to enjoy, in this day and age, the old atmosphere, so rare in its reality, closeness and continuity, and to walk in the narrow and steep streets. Paved with slabs of stone between high buildings, small squares and yards and sudden steep bifurcations, the rich artistic inheritance, resulting from the town liberality and the power of the banking companie and the merchants, displays the mo splendid moment of the town in th magic «Trecento Senese» (Siena durin the 14th century) during which magnif cent and continuous examples of a chitecture, painting and sculptu flourished, that are still extremely we preserved and that represent the best c 14th century Italian artistic productio

THE HISTORY OF THE TOWN

The origin of the town dates back t the legends of its foundation attribu ed now to the Senones Gauls, then Remo's son Senio from whom the tow takes the symbol of the Roman sh wolf. It is certain the Etruscans settle in a place called Sena; we are less ce tain that the Gauls settled there aft the 5th century B.C. invasion. In th Republican period Siena became R man and Emperor Augustus place there a military colony bearing th name of Sena Julia. In the Middle Ag we can already foresee the beginning the wealth of the town ruled by the f mily of Gastaldi, and then by the f mily of Conti in the Carolingian Ag The bishops exercised such a stro power in the 10th and 11th centuri that the mighty landowners were forc to submit to them. Then, the citize progressively grew economically a

politically and the laical power of the consuls came to reverse the bishops' secular power. Siena began to expand its dominion over the owners of the surrounding lands operating in Ghibelline rivalry against the Guelph Florence. At first the disputes against the empire (A.D. 1186 Henry, son of Red-Beard, laid siege to the town), then the submission to Otto the Fourth underlined the commercial interests of Siena, whose merchants were present everywhere in Europe and soon would have become the Pope's bankers. This politic situation secured the permanent hostility of the neighbouring feudatories and of the powerful Florence. These two powers tried everything to break down Sienese commercial activities, until the bloody battle against the Florentine that cost Siena the towns of Poggibonsi and Montalcino (A.D. 1235).

In 1236 a council of 24 members replaced the noblemen supremacy: there were 12 noblemen and 12 middle-class members, the latter being powerful by then, owing to the wealth of trades and arts. Very soon, however, the rivalry with Florence blew up again; in fact Florence was looking for a route to the sea and the hostility was almost softened by the occupation of Pisa, an important target (A.D. 1254). A new attempt by Florence against Siena failed miserably causing enormous losses (10,000 people died and 15,000 were taken as prisoners) on September 4, 1280 A.D., in the epic battle of Montaperti.

There followed a decade full of flourishing studies and arts for the town; nevertheless the triumph of the Ghibelline party cost Siena, which had replaced the consular power with a Podestà (a prefect) supported by a People's Captain, a papal ex-communica-

1. Panoramic view of the Cathedral and the Tower of Mangia; 2. Aerial view of Piazza del Campo; 3. She-wolf feeding the twins, work in gold-plated tin by Giovanni di Turino, in the Municipal Museum.

3

tion and consequent serious difficulties in trading. The merchants went over to the Guelph Party and, in the town, disputes between noblemen and the lower classes blew up. After being defeated in Monteriggioni (A.D. 1269) the power of the town began to slide into Guelph politics and there was an agreement with Florence, at first creating a council of 36 representatives of all parties, then of 15 (A.D. 1280) following on the Government of the Nine which held power till the 1355. This government, Guelph, lower class — and merchants — oriented, guaranteed the town the richest period in its history, providing it with magnificent monuments and buildings.

The wars, famines (A.D. 1326), and pestilences (A.D. 1348) menaced the Government of the Nine which was overthrown by the noblemen, supported by the Emperor Charles the Fourth, in 1355. Different forms of government followed on, but none of them was able to re-establish political stability in the town till the moment when, in 1399, Gian Galeazzo Visconti, Duke of Milan, was proclaimed the Prince of Siena. When he died in 1404, Siena again claimed its freedom, assigning to itself a government of 10 Priors. During this long historical period of political weakness and wars, the voices of peace of St. Catherine (A.D. 1347-1380) and of St. Bernardino (A.D. 1380-1444) were raised, while a man from Siena, Silvio Piccolomini, became Pope assuming the name of Pius the Second (A.D. 1458). In the heat of revolts, expulsions and banning orders, the figure of Pandolfo Petrucci, who controlled the government from A.D. 1487 to the 1512 prevailed, ensuring a brief period of stability and growth. On his death Siena fell again into political chaos till the entry into the town of the imperial troops of Charles the Fifth, King of Spain, in 1530. From then on the interests of the greatest European powers prevailed over the town. In A.D. 1552 the inhabitants of Siena revolted and succeeded in chasing the Spaniards out, war broke out and in 1554 Siena was laid siege to by Spaniards, Germans and Italians lead by Gian Giacomo de' Medici. After a heroic but vain resistance the town fell on April 17, 1555. The treaty of Cateau-Cambrésis stated that the town and all its dominions passed to Cosimo the First. Together with the whole of Tuscany then, Siena passed from the Medici Family to the house of Lorena. Under Napoleonic domination Siena was, briefly, chief town of the district of Ombrone before returning to the house of Lorena till the «risorgimento»: Siena was the first town in Tuscany to be annexed to the Reign of Italy (1859).

ART

The artistic patrimony of the town, bound up mainly with the liberality and wealth of the merchant classes which considered it, not only a symbol of political autonomy, but also an attribute of dignity, can be concentrated in a brief lapse of time beginning from the 12th century. Several buildings, towers and small pure Romanesque churches belong to this period (San Donato, San Pietro alla Magione, San Cristoforo, San Marco, San Quirico).

1

The transition between Romanesque and Gothic architecture is characterized by the building of the «Duomo» (cathedral) and lasted two centuries. The artistic fever which contributed to make the town flourish in the urbanistic field and in the civil and ecclesiastic architecture, which we can still admire, was focused on this constructions. This fervour renders Sienese Gothic similar to the Tuscan but at the same time different because it is more decorative and daring.

The façade, the apse and the upper part of the middle nave of the cathedral, the baptistry, the new cathedral, the churches of San Francesco, San Domenico and Santa Maria dei Servi, belong to this Gothic period. In the civil works Sienese architecture differs from the Gothic patterns common with other towns and finds its highest characterization in the construction of the «Public Building», completed in the middle of the 14th century, whose building elements are revised with harmony of inspiration, in other buildings of that period (Sansedoni building, Chigi-Saracini building, the building of the Captain) or of following ages (Marsili building, Buonsignori building). Furthermore, the Sienese architectural peculiarity spread other elements such as the fountains, the gates and the walls. In the 15th century the prevailing work of Florentine architects introduced to the town Renaissance architecture: Piccolomini buildings, the Papesse building, Ugurgieri building, and Spannocchi building all belong to this period, as do the work of Antonio Federighi (Pope's loggias, the Chapel in the square, building and Chapel of the Diavoli) and Francesco di Giorgio Martini, both from Siena.

The 16th century is dominated by the figure of Baldassarre Peruzzi who worked, however, for the most part, out of the town.

Other churches belong to the Baroque age: Santa Maria di Provenzano, a work of Damiano Schifardini; Santi Pietro e Paolo, a work of Flaminio del Turco and San Martino, a work of Giovanni Fontana.

In the field of sculpture the figure of Jacopo della Quercia is outstanding. Thanks to him Sienese sculpture reached the highest peaks of success (Fonte Gaia, the Gay Fountain; Fonte Battesimale, the Baptism Fountain); the Siena school owes its birth to the

1. Detail of the battle of the Sienese represented in the frescoes over the arches in the Hall of the Map of the World in the Municipal Museum; 2. Detail of the rowers of the «Battle between the Venetians and the Imperials in Punta Salvatore», by Spinello Aretino. Hall of Balia in the Municipal Museum; 3. Panoramic view of the Sanctuary of Saint Catherine.

work of Nicola and Giovanni Pisano. Nicola produced the cathedral pulpit while Giovanni built the façade.

The most important expression in the Sienese artistic field, however, is painting. Guido da Siena is the first one of the group of great painters working in Siena, his «Madonna» in the Public Building dates back to the second half of the 13th century. Duccio di Buoninsegna, the next artist who worked with talent and skill in the Gothic age, is considered the great founder of the school.

2

Following on, there are the works of Simone Martini, of Lorenzetti and his disciples, Barna, Lippo Vanni, Taddeo di Bartolo, Jacopo di Mino del Pellicciaio and Paolo di Giovanni Fei. In the 15th century some works stand out: Sassetta's, Domenico di Bartolo's and the works of Sano di Pietro, Vecchietta, Giovanni di Paolo, Matteo di Giovanni. In the following century we find Sodoma, Domenico Beccafumi and Baldassarre Peruzzi.

In the following ages we no longer find very valuable masters. Also, among the minor arts, Siena could give great importance to the ability of its own craftsmen who worked with perfection and decorative elegance in the goldsmith's art, in marquetry and in miniature.

This artistic panorama, so wide and various, makes the town worth the appellation «Town of Art», with its fascinating medieval integrity which lights up again the feasts and the wealth of that age, from the impressive atmosphere of its streets to the explosive scenery of Palio colours and passions.

1. The effects of Good Government, by A. Lorenzetti (Hall of Peace in the Municipal Museum); 2. Virgin with Child, work by Duccio di Buoninsegna (Museum of the Cathedral); 3. Architectural detail of the Cathedral; on page 8, panoramic view of the city.

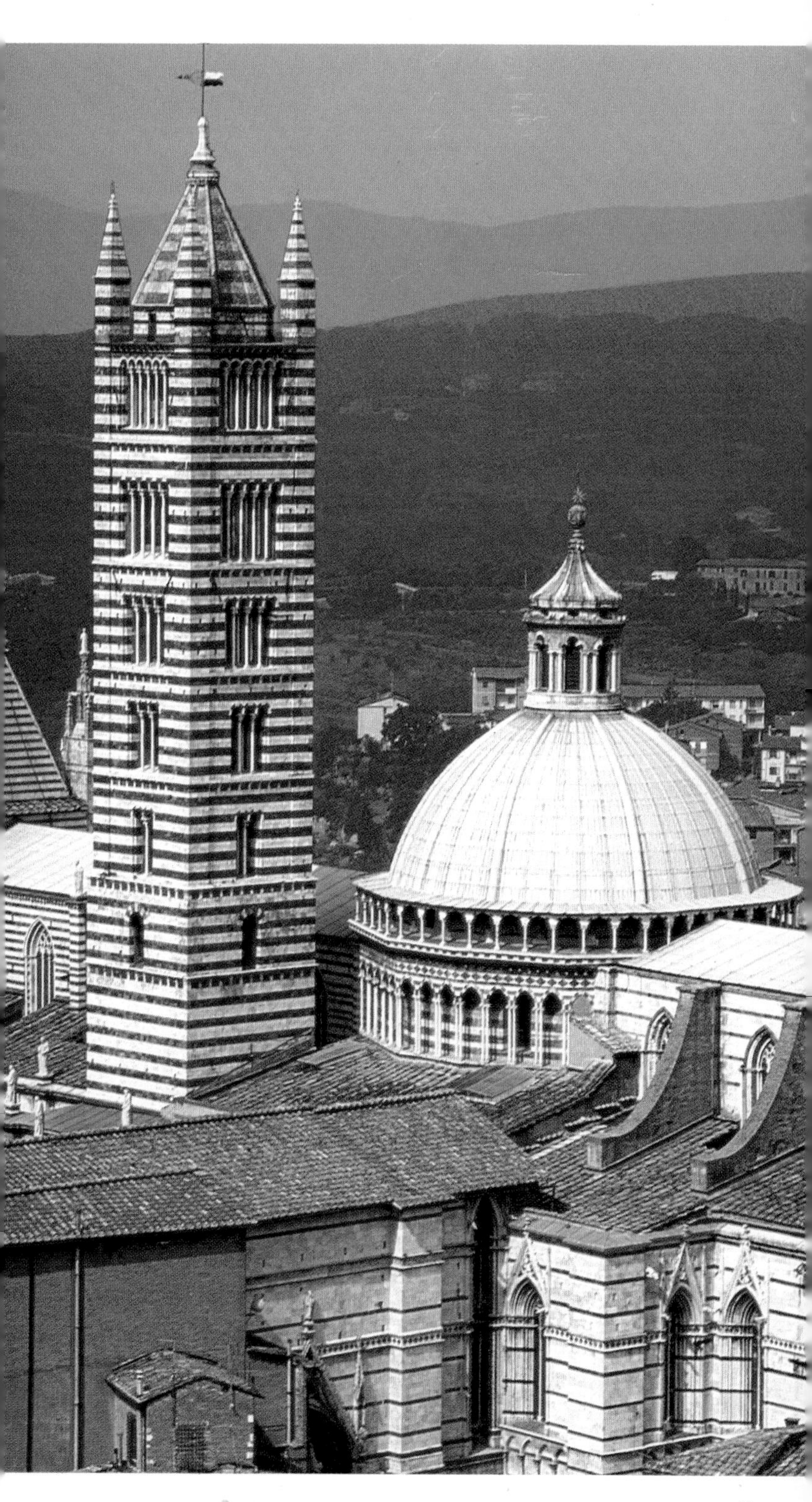

TOUR OF THE TOWN NO. ONE

1

Loggia of the Merchants • Campo Square • Gaia Fountain • Palazzo Pubblico • Mangia Tower • Chapel of the Square • Interior Palazzo Pubblico • Civic Museum • Yard of the Podestà • Palazzi around the Campo Square

LOGGIA OF THE MERCHANTS

The middle of the town is considered to be the crossing — called Cross of the Troubles (Croce del Travaglio) — of the streets of the town, Banchi di Sotto e Banchi di Sopra. In the Middle Ages in this place the hostile parties gathered for struggling and the site became a border zone, barricaded or blocked.

Very nearby is the Loggia della Mercanzia or dei Mercanti (of the merchants), also called Loggia di San Paolo.

In 1417 Sano di Matteo realized the project of this small building whose style wavers between Gothic and Renaissance. In 1444 Pietro del Minella completed the construction. The height of this severe and solid building, composed of three arcades, was increased by one storey in 17th century. It has been the seat of the commercial court of justice but is now the seat of the «Circolo degli Uniti» (Union Club) and the Province Tourist Board. We find on the pillars, inside the Gothic tabernacles, statues of Saints by Vecchietta and Antonio Federighi. The iron gate dates back to 1887. Inside there are two marble slabs: the right one, representing five Oromani figures was made by Federighi (1464), the other is by Urbano da Cortona. Pastorino dei Pastorini, together with Lorenzo Rustici painted, between 1549 and 1563, the frescoes and the stuccoes of the vaults.

On the left of the Loggia are to be noticed an old tower-house and a small construction with a twice-mullioned window of the 14th century. In this way we arrive at the San Pietro Lane, through which you get to Piazza del Campo.

SQUARE OF THE CAMPO (FIELD)

The square is the most famous monument of Siena: it is the real centre of the town, placed between the ridge lines of the three hills over which it stands. Its peculiar shape, a fan-basin, almost a shell, is famous all over the world for creating a special scenic effect, making this square a masterpiece of beauty. The perimeter edge is flag-stoned; since 1347 the interior fan has been made of bricks subdivided into 9 sectors by stone courses. The nine sectors are to recollect the Government of Nine; in fact it was during that period the square and the Public Building were built.

1

1. Loggia of the Merchants; 2. Piazza del Campo.

In this splendid scenery surrounded by old buildings and monuments, seat of the «Palio», Siena has enjoyed the most dramatic and joyful moments of its history.

GAIA FOUNTAIN

In the middle of the square, on the top of the brick-paved hemicycle, there is the Fonte Gaia. It was built between 1409 and 1419, on the same site as an old 14th century fountain by Jacopo della Quercia, master of the art in Siena. He lived between 1374 and 1438. The original bas-reliefs are preserved in the Public Building and the one in the square are replacement copies made by Tito Sarocchio in 1868.

PUBLIC BUILDING

On the opposite side to the fountain, the scenery of the square is obscured by the Public Building. This is a splendid and harmonic pattern of Tuscan Gothic building. It was built to be the seat of the «Signoria» (government) and of the Podestà and today has become the municipal residence. On its side we find the tower of Mangia and the Chapel of the Square. The building represents the most remarkable example of formal elegance in Sienese Gothic architecture. The whole lightness and the ardour of the town's architectural language are well represented by this construction: the building of its oldest part was completed in 1310. The prisons and the Hall of the Great Council were built enlarging the right side between 1327 and 1342. It is composed of a central body and two side wings bent into a slight arch, the second floor of which is a result of an increasing of height which occurred in 1680.

The ground floor, built with stones, has windows and doors, enclosed and decorated with the characteristic Sienese arch. On the upper floors, made of bricks, there are two series of twice-mullioned windows and one series of mullioned ones. The cornice of the central body is placed on small arches and surrounded with battlements, in the same way as the side bodies, on which the small arches are based on the marcapiano of the ground floor. On the top there are two bell cells. In the middle of the last floor has been placed a great disc having in its centre a monogram of Jesus Christ painted by Battista di Nicolò in 1425; on its sides there are two stone she-wolves. Among the twice-mullioned windows on the first floor there is the Medici symbol (1560), a slab representing the Sienese coat of arms, half white and half black, and the lion of the People.

P

2

TOWER OF MANGIA

On the left of the building the elegant and slender form of the tower of Mangia stands out: it is in fact 88 metres high, including the battlements. The name derives from Giovanni di Duccio, called the Earnings-eater (Mangiaguadagni) or simply the Mangia, who was one of the tower's first bell-ringers. The name was inherited by the automaton that, till 1780, had the same functions. The work was by the brothers Minuccio di Rinaldo who built it between 1338 and 1348. Above the brick trunk there is a harmonius crown of long stone bartizans. The bell tower designed by Lippo Memmi (1341) was made of the same material.

3

THE CHAPEL OF THE SQUARE

On the same side of the tower, leaning on the left wing of the Public Building, we find the stone construction of the Chapel of the Square. The construction, which took place between 1352 and 1376 by Domenico di Agostino, plan designer, and was completed by Giovanni di Cecco, is dedicated to the fulfilling of a vow expressed by the people of Siena during the plague of 1348. It was accomplished, according to its present shape, adding Renaissance arches and the covering vault by Antonio Federighi (1468). Between 1377 and 1381 the decoration of the pillars with figured statues of Saints was completed.

The balustrade marbles are school of Pisa bas-reliefs of the 13th century appropriated from another monument.

1. Public Palace and Tower of Mangia; 2. Gaia Fountain; 3. Piazza Chapel.

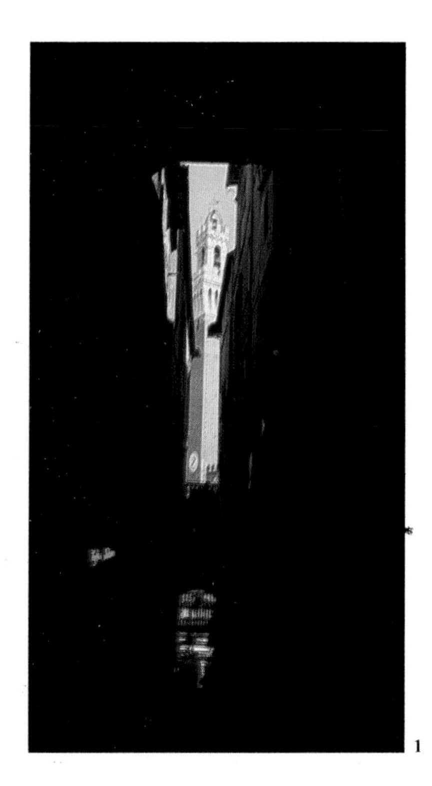

1. *View of the Tower of Mangia.*

INTERIOR OF THE PUBLIC BUILDING

We enter the Public Building through the right portal: after crossing the first entrance-hall we arrive at the vestibule, subdivided into four spans; on the walls we can see two 14th century stone wolves and some stone gargoyles, ascribed to Giovanni Pisano; a small statue by Antonio Federighi representing «Moses», and a fresco, painted by Sano di Pietro in 1446, representing the Saints and the Blessed Souls Pietro Alessandrino, Ambrogio Sansedoni and Andrea Gallerani, can also be seen. On the sides of the vestibule there are halls which now are used as municipal offices: the hall of the Major in which has been preserved a remarkable Madonna con Bambino (Virgin with the Holy Child) and the Saints Giovannino, Michele and Galgano, painted by Sodoma in 1537. The vault is decorated with 17th century frescoes: the waiting hall or Biccherna hall, decorated with a wonderful fresco by Sano di Pietro in 1445, representing the coronation of the Virgin Mary, the angels and the Saints Bernardino and Catherine of Siena. The vault is covered with 17th century frescoes, the furniture is an inlaid bench cover of the 15th century, the office halls of the General Secretery have a fresco by Sodoma (1535), they also have the Resurrection and a Virgin with San Sebastiano painted on a standard by Arcangelo Salimbeni. On the opposite side of the vestibule there is the former wedding hall, having on its external side a fresco of the Imperial Eagle and two Putti (children) painted by Sodoma, and containing on its internal side a large fresco: Virgin of mercy and Santi Bernardino and Michele, by Vecchietta (1461); the hall, identified as the old Chapel of the Nine, having on the ceiling a Blessing Christ among cherubims by Simone Martini, the Evangelists by Lorenzo Veneziano, the Blessed Soul Andrea Gallerani, Sant'Antonio Abate and an Annunciation by Andrea Vanni (1370).

THE CIVIC MUSEUM

Going up from the entrance hall we can visit the Civic Museum on the first floor. We enter the Globe Hall after crossing the Vestibule in which are preserved a she-wolf suckling the twins in golden metal, by Giovanni Turino (1429-1430), and a Virgin Mary with the Child, what remains of a larger fresco by Ambrogio Lorenzetti (1340). The name of the **hall is taken from rotating globe** of the Siena territory made by Ambrogio Lorenzetti in the beginning of the 14th century, now unfortunately lost. In this hall we can admire the great fresco of the **Majesty**, by Simone Martini, the first certain painting of his, in 1315. The grand and very famous work represents the Virgin with the Child on the throne below a golden canopy propped up by eight Apostles, at the foot of the throne there are angels, Saints and other Apostles: in total there are 32 figures painted posed in a noble attitude. The sweetness of the figures, the almost ethereal quality of the canopy, the flowing harmony of the composition, put this work at the height of Gothic art, wisely permeating the utmost artistic and decorative sense of the author. The work is completed by a large frame containing 20 medallions on which there are the image of Christ, the Prophets, the Evangelists and the Doctors of the Church, the Old and the New Law (figure with two faces) and finally, the seal of the Republic. Humidity made the first restoration necessary just six years later by the same author and, unfortunately, the damage wrought has vitiated it as a work of art. On the opposite side we admire another fresco by Simone Martini «**Guidoriccio da Fogliano** between the castles of Montemassi and Sassoforte of Maremma» (1328); also this work fixes the mastery of the author over the subject, represented with monumental splendour, and shows a great sense of decorative and airy scenes in painting a moment of the medieval life in the courts.

On the other walls of the hall we can see: among the arcades, above, two monochrome frescoes; The Victory of Siena over Florence at Poggio Imperiale, by Giovanni di Cristoforo and Francesco d'Andrea (1480) and the Victory of Siena, headed by Giordano d'Orsini, over the English company of the Hat, headed by Niccolò di Montefeltro in Asinalunga or in Torrita di Val di Chiana (1363), painted by Lippo Vanni; below, on the pillars, other figures are represented: from the right, The Blessed Souls Andrea Gallerani and Ambrogio Sansedoni (17th century), Saint Catherine of Siena, by Vecchietta (1461), San Bernardino by Sano di Pietro (1460) and The Blessed Soul Bernardo Tolomei by Sodoma (1533).

Below the fresco of Guidoriccio, in the middle we find a board painted by Guido da Siena, The Virgin with the Child on the Throne, which dates

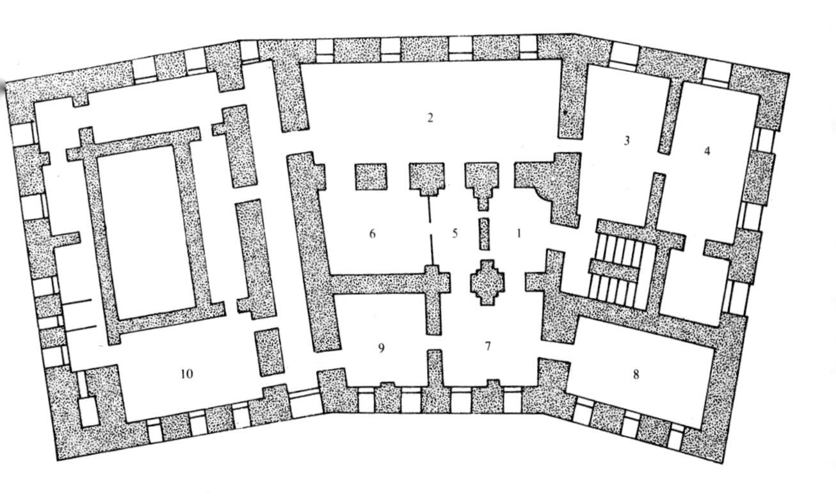

PALAZZO PUBBLICO (PUBLIC BUILDING): CIVIC MUSEUM, FIRST FLOOR

1 . Entrance Hall
2 . The Map Hall
3 . Hall of Peace or of the Nine
4 . Hall of Pillars
5 . Antechapel
6 . Chapel
7 . Hall of the Cardinals
8 . Hall of the Consistory
9 . Balia or the Priors's Hall
10 . Hall of the Risorgimento

back to 1221, but is attributed by the critics to the second half of the 13th century: this work, very important for being a witness to the first moments of the Siena painting school, was touched up by Duccio or one of his disciples, who made small changes to the head and to the hands of the Virgin and the Child.

On the sides of The Majesty we find two monumental frescoes by Sodoma: San Vittore, on the right, and Sant'Ansano giving baptism, on the left (1529).

From the Globe Hall, turning right we get into the **Hall of Peace or the Hall of the Nine**, in which the Government of the Nine had its site. In this hall we can admire one of the most famous cycles of profane frescoes of the Middle Ages. It was made by Ambrogio Lorenzetti between

3

1337 and 1339; the fresco carries out, using moral, political and didactic references, three allegorical subjects: the Good Government, the Effects of the Good Government in the town and in the countryside, and the Bad Government and its effects. The three subjects are represented very vividly and sharply. In the Good Government fresco, on the wall in front of the window, is represented an old king, wearing black and white clothes (the colours of Siena flag), having on his left Magnanimity, Temperance and Justice, on his right Prudence, Strength and Peace. Over the king the three theological virtues are flying about: Faith, Hope and Charity, at his foot the she-wolf suckles the twins Aschilo and Senio, mythical founders of the town, and further to the right the Sienese army is taking prisoners. On the left side we see Justice, her face looking at Wisdom over her, propping up a pair of scales with which two angels administer the commutative and distributive justice. Under Justice, Concord sits back, having in her hands two ropes coming from the scales of the balance and on her knees the

1.2. Hall of the Map of the World, with frescoes; 3. The great fresco of the Majesty by Simone Martini; 4. The Majesty (detail).

4

plane, levelling all human ambitions.

On the entrance hall wall there is a representation of the effects of Good Government in the town and in the countryside: the view of Siena in the 14th century, towers and buildings, knights on their horses in streets and squares, dancing girls and pedlars enlivening the calmness of the daily life, while the country view, among mountains, woods and hills shows the fervour of activities such as reaping, ploughing, fishing and hunting. On the opposite wall is represented the Bad Government and its effects through the allegory of Tyranny having her feet on a black goat, sitting among Cruelty, Deceit,

Fury, Discord and Wickedness. Above this scene there are Miserliness, Arrogance and Vainglory, while Justice is beaten and in chains.

Crossing the Hall of Peace we enter the **Hall of Pillars**. Here some things are preserved: a small board painted on the two sides, representing the Sermon of San Bernardino and San Bernardino exorcising a devil from a possessed woman, made by Neroccio di Bartolomeo Landi, a fresco representing the Saints Stefano, Maddalena and Antonio, a work by the Sienese School (end of the 14th century), an Annunciation, which dates back to the same period, a Virgin Mary with the Child, by Duccio's School. Inside some glass show-cases we find a wooden chest with the figures of the Siena Patron Saints (end of the 14th century), a coffer of the 15th century, a wooden chest inlaid by Antonio Barili and the bell of the San Cristoforo Church. The bell is preserved here because it was tolled to gather the troops for the battle of Montaperti.

Returning from the Globe Hall we enter the ante-chapel, decorated with frescoes representing scenes of Roman history and of Greek-Roman mythology, painted by Taddeo di Bartolo (1407-1414). The same author made the San Cristoforo on the opposite wall, while the small, wooden statue representing San Nicola of Bari has been attributed to Antonio Federighi. Beside it we find a **chapel** barred by a heavy gate made of tinned wrought-iron built by Giacomo di Giovanni and his son Giovanni in 1437 (probably the plan and the design were by Jacopo della Quercia). The furniture is: a hanging holy water basin in gilded bronze by Giovanni di Turino (1434); a rich wooden chandelier, painted and gilded, Gothic style (1370); the organ in inlaid wood, a late-Renaissance work of Giovanni di Pietro and Ghino d'Antonio (1524); along the wall there is a wooden choir composed of 22 high-backed chairs inlaid in Gothic style by Domenico di Niccolò between 1415 and 1428. The panels

of the backs have figurations whose inspiration was drawn from the Credo, and thus was the author subsequently called Domenico of the Choirs. The marble altar is by Marrina and above it there is a Sodoma's board representing the Holy Family and San Leonardo (first half of the 16th century); on the vaults and on the walls there are frescoes by Bartolo (first half of the 15th century) representing figures drawn from the story of the Virgin Mary and other religious subjects, Evangelists, Prophets, Doctors of the Church.

From the Anti-chapel we move towards the **Cardinal's Hall** decorated with: in the entrance, a 14th century board with the painting of a crucifix; a tabernacle, on the division pillars, by Guidoccio Cozzarelli who painted on it a Virgin Mary with the Child and angels; on the right, two wooden plastered statues of Sant'Antonio Abate and Sant'Ambrogio, probably made by Antonio Federighi, a disciple of Jacopo della Quercia: on the wall a fresco of three Saints and a devotee on his knees, attributed to Ambrogio Lorenzetti; above as on the other wall, the figures of Saints frescoed in the 14th and 15th centuries.

1. Guidoriccio da Fogliano, work by Simone Martini.

From this point going towards the left we enter the **hall of «Consistory»**. The marble portal is an elegant work by Bernardo Rossellino (1448), while the shutters in inlaid wood were made by Domenico di Niccolò. The vault, frescoed with allegories of heroic episodes of Greek and Roman history according to Valerio Massimo, was completed by Domenico Beccafumi, nicknamed «Mecarino», between 1529 and 1535: in the centre we recognize Justice, Concord, Patriotism: over the portal there is a painting by Luca Giordano, The Judgement of Solomon. Finally, on the walls, there are three large pieces of tapestry coming from the Gobelins

3

fabrics, The Allegory of the Earth, of the Air, and of the Fire, designed by Charles le Brun (17th century), and five smaller pieces of tapestry (16th century) made in Florence.

Coming back and crossing the Cardinal's hall we enter **the hall of Balia or the Hall of the Priors**. This hall, in which the Council of the Magistrates held their meetings, is totally frescoed and is divided into two

1.2. Hall of Peace. «The effects of Good Government in town and country»; 3. «The effects of Bad Government», works by A. Lorenzetti; 4. The Chapel; 5. Hall of Balia.

parts by an arch. The vaults were painted by the Sienese painter Martino di Bartolomeo, between 1407 and 1408: he subdivided the ceiling into 16 triangular sectors and in each of them he depicted a Virtue. In the arch which crosses the hall there are the figures of the Evangelists, six busts of emperors and warriors and, on the pilasters, other figures of Virtues. On the walls, in a cycle of episodes, is represented the story of the Pope Alexander the Third, Rolando Bandinelli from Siena, who lived in the 12th century and fought against the Emperor Red-Beard: the work is one of the last by Spinello Aretino with the help of his son, Parri, in 1408.

The door in inlaid wood is by

Domenico di Niccolò, the inlaid bench by Barna di Turino (1410). Going out of the hall of Balia we enter, from the landing of the huge stairway which leads to the upper floors, the **hall of Risorgimento** (a period of Italian history in the 19th century), where many works by artists from Siena and Tuscany of the end of the 19th century are preserved. In the five halls surrounding the yard of Podestà we find a collection of artistic works of small size and a remarkable collection of coins and medals.

Going up the stairway, on the first flight, we enter three halls in which are placed lime casts of the most important works of Jacopo della Quercia: among them the portal of the Church of San Petronio in Bologna and the sepulchre of Ilaria del Carretto in Lucca. The last flight of the stairway brings us to the entrance of the **Loggia**, erected on 4 pillars, opening onto the market square and the valley east of the town. Here experts have re-assembled the original bas-reliefs and the sculptures made by Jacopo della Quercia for the Gaia fountain between 1409 and 1419. In spite of the corrosion provoked by the flow of time the works display the great artistic skill of the master.

From the Loggia we get to the **Big Hall of the Signoria**, actually of th Municipal Council. In it we find tw canvasses, painted by Amos Cassio li, The Oath in Pontida and Proven zano Salvani in the Square of th Campo in Siena, and in the vault lu nettes, Sienese tales made by artist in the end of the 16th century. In th other halls on the second floor ther are various works, among which th striking ones are: a collection o prints (by Jacques Callof and Stefan della Bella), 17th and 18th centurie canvasses, portraits of notables, ge ographical maps and plenty of docu ments referring to the history of th town and its urban plan, and th Palio.

On the upper floor, called La Mar colina, intended for enlarging th Civic Museum, we discover that th great fresco detached from th Chapel of the Square, Virgin Mary Saints and the Holy Father, a work of 1539 by Sodoma, has been pre served here since 1973.

YARD OF PODESTÀ

Through a door of the Public Building close to the Chapel of th Square we get to the Yard of Pode stà, built in 1325 and restored in 1929. It is a brick-work constructio with a portico in the ground floo and an upper floor opened out by ample lancet twice-mullioned win dows. Aligned on the walls there ar several symbols of the Podestà an moreover a fresco of Virgin Mary with the angels, of the 14th century and a statue by Mangia. At the bot tom of the hall a door leads to th Municipal Theatre of the Rinnovat (Renewed): once the old Hall of th Great Council of the Republic, the adapted to become Theatre of th Hedgehog, rebuilt in 1560 after be ing damaged by two fires by the Bib biena in 1753 and, finally, restore in 1951. The hall appears to be com

1. Loggia of the Public Palace. Origina sculpture made by Jacopo della Quercia fo the Gaia Fountain; 2. Courtyard of th Podestà; 3. View from the courtyard of th Podestà; 4. Sansedoni Palace.

3

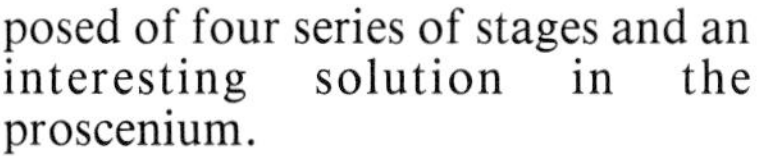

posed of four series of stages and an interesting solution in the proscenium.

Another door in the yard lets onto the stairway which arrives at the top of the **Tower of Mangia**. After climbing 332 steps we arrive at the bell frame, melted in 1665 by Girolamo Santoni from Fano and Giovanni Battista Salvini from Siena, nicknamed the Big Bell or Sunto, because it was dedicated to the Virgin Mary received into Heaven (Maria Assunta). From here you can enjoy the magnificent view of the town with its monuments and the surrounding gentle hills.

THE BUILDINGS OF PIAZZA DEL CAMPO

On the Piazza del Campo we have the possibility, turning our eyes towards the ample semi-circle of buildings, of admiring the impressive architectural harmony. Their homogeneity is due to the constant care the old rulers took, already in the statutes of 1309, in giving wise dispositions about every aspect of the buildings in the square: they forbade galleries, penthouses and jutties on the façades and the only windows allowed were the two and three mullioned windows. These careful or-

dinances allow us to enjoy a wing of buildings admirably in harmony with the magic basin of the square.

Going round the square starting from the corner of the Tower of Mangia, at the end of the semi-circle where Rinaldini Street makes its way into the square, there is the *Chigi-Zondadari Building*. The building rebuilt in 1724 by Antonio Valeri dates back to an old age.

Following on there is the big *Sansedoni Building*. The origin of the edifice can be traced back to 1216 from an aggregation of buildings which Agostino di Giovanni arranged in 1339 operating amplifications and changes. The actual façade in Piazza del Campo is due to a reconstruction executed during the first years of the 18th century, when the whole complex was unified into a court residence. The fundamental elements of this majestic piece of architecture are: three series of three mullioned windows, the battlement and the tower, having a rhomboid plan with twice-mullioned windows. All these elements are made of bricks. The tower, once higher than today, the disposition of the windows, the upper cornices and the curving shape remind us clearly of the architectural image of the Public Building. Inside the building, on the ceiling of some halls, frescoes of Gian Domenico Ferretti (1745-1760) are left.

The rear of the Loggia della Mercanzia façade is placed between two lanes: San Paolo and San Pietro. It was rebuilt in 1763, designed by Ferdinando Fuga.

Following on we find the houses De Metz, on whose façades we see traces of lancet openings.

Getting over the Costarella (small slope) dei Barbieri, we see the *Elci's Building*, which stands out among the others in this block. It is a high building with battlement which dates back to the 16th century. Walking on we arrive at the path leading to the characteristic «chiasso del Bargello».

2

1.2. The palaces of Piazza del Campo; 3. Via di Città and Chigi-Saracini Palace; 4. Chigi-Saracini Palace: courtyard and stone well.

TOUR OF THE TOWN NO. TWO

Chigi-Saracini Palace • Piccolomini Palace • Marsili Palace • Postierla Square • Capitano Palace • Square of the Duomo (Cathedral) • Cathedral • New Cathedral • Cathedral Museum • Crypt • Baptistery • Hospital of Santa Maria della Scala • Archbishop's Palace • San Sebastiano in Valle Piatta

Walking up along Via di Città towards the Cathedral Square, on the left can be seen the Square of the Campo of which one can enjoy picturesque views through the Costarella dei Barbieri and the lane of the Bargello. Then one follows an evocative medieval itinerary among important architectural examples: towers, tower-houses, small palaces and noble palaces.

On the other corner on the side of Barbieri stands a stone tower, called the Tower of the Seven Seghinelle, a portion of the old Crocini Palace: it opens on to the street with stone-mullioned windows inserted in ogival arches. Moving on, at No. 75, there is the *Patrizi Palace*, a 14th century brickwork construction, seat of the Academy of Intronati.

CHIGI-SARACINI PALACE

At No. 89 of Via di Città one finds the Chigi-Saracini Palace. Long ago this construction was the Marescotti Palace, initiated in the 12th century and repeating the usual scheme carried out in Siena of the palace with a tower in the corner. It was completed during the first half of the 14th century, adjusted in the 18th century and restored between 1914 and 1922. Its façade, broken in order to follow the curve of the street, has

3

been built with stone in the lower part and with bricks in the upper floor: the tower, on the left, is made of stone too. The ogival arches encompass wide windows and main doors on the ground floor, two lines of twice-mullioned windows in the upper floor: the upper frames and the battlements are of bricks. The building, following the will of the Count Guido Chigi Saracini, has been, since 1932, the seat of the *Chigi Musical Academy*, today acknowledged as an important centre of musical perfection which, among other things, organizes, every July, the «Siena Musical Week» with artists drawing an international public. From the dark lobby in which there is a statue of Giulio the Third by Fulvio Signorini (1609) one comes to the yard, partly porticoed and with a stone well. From here one enters the first floor and a series of sumptuous halls, the most interesting one being the 18th century style *Concert hall*, frescoed by Arturo Villigiardi: the subject is the Return from the Battle of Montaperti.

In the building there is also a rich gallery with remarkable works of Sienese art from the 14th century: a marble bas-relief, attributed uncertainly to Donatello or Vecchietta; a wooden polychrome statue of The Deposition and some sketches of the Gaia fountain by Jacopo della Quercia; a crucifix by the Berlinghieri School and one by the Giotto School; a San Paolo by Simone Martini and three paintings by Sassetta, The Epiphany, the Virgin Mary and San Giovanni, San Martino; a Virgin Mary with Child by Matteo di Giovanni and one by Neroccio di Bartolomeo; a Virgin Mary with Child and Angels by Botticelli, an Infant Jesus by Perugino and many other works by Lorenzo di Credi, Sebastiano del Piombo, Pontormo, Sodoma, Beccafumi and other artists. Also extremely interesting is a collection of musical instruments.

PICCOLOMINI PALACE

Not far from the Chigi-Saracini Palace, at No. 126, there is the Piccolomini Palace, also called the Palace of the Female Popes (delle Papesse) at present seat of the Bank of Italy. It was built between 1460 and 1495, probably from a plan by Bernardo Rossellino, for Caterina Piccolomini, sister of the Pope Pius the Second. It underwent several restorations, the last one in 1864 by Augusto Corbi. It is a typical exam-

1

le of Florentine Renaissance architecture: rustic ashral-work on the round floor and on the upper floors vo lines of mullioned windows. The alace shows traces of the typical ienese architecture, especially in the se of Gothic-style elements.

ARSILI PALACE

At the corner between Via di Cit-a and Castoro Street there is the Marsili Palace. It was built halfway rough the 15th century by Luca di artolo. It is constructed completely of brickwork and the façade is dorned with three lines of twice-mullioned windows. Also remarkable is the sail-vault lobby and Renaissance style corbels.

OSTIERLA SQUARE

Walking on along Via di Città to ie Postierla Square one arrives at an ld tower-house on the right, the *Forteguerri house*. In the square, called ie Four Districts Square, there is a olumn, which has on the top of it marble Sienese she-wolf (1487) and a 15th century wrought-iron flag-bearer.

At the corner between the square and Capitano Street rises the Chigi alla Postierla Palace: it is a good example of 16th century building and was attributed to Riccio; it houses, on the inside, two halls frescoed by the Flemish painter Bernardo van Rantwyck with stuccoes by Marcello Sparti.

4

. Via di Città with Palazzo Piccolomini, lso called of the «female Popes», and the alazzo Chigi-Saracini; 2. Side view from anchi di Sopra; 3. Postierla square; 4. Side iew of the characteristic Via della Galluzza.

PALACE OF THE CAPITANO

Walking up towards the Cathedral along Capitano Street one finds at No. 15, the huge Palace of the Captain of the People. The name derives from the fact that it was the old seat of the Captain of Justice and then became first the property of the Grottanelli family, then of Pecci's and finally of the Piccolomini's: since 1963 to the present day, it has been the seat of the Faculty of Economics and Banking Sciences. It was built between the 13th and 14th centuries with typically Gothic architectural characteristics: ogival arches, mullioned windows, embattled cornices. In the 15th century the building underwent a transforming operation by Luca di Bartolo which gave it a Renaissance look but, in 1864, it was restored and brought back into the previous style.

CATHEDRAL SQUARE

Going out from Capitano Street and entering the Cathedral Square one can admire the splendid succession of buildings facing the square: in the left is the Hospital of Santa Maria della Scala; at the bottom is the Archbishop's Palace and th Cathedral; on the right the arcade of the New Cathedral and the Palac of the Prefect.

THE CATHEDRAL

The historical events. In the firs half of the 12th century constructio began on the Siena Cathedral, dedi cated to Our Lady. Very little i known about this period and the lon and troubled events of its construc tion. At the beginning of the histor of the Commune of Siena the con struction was financed by the Tow Council which, to begin with, was en trusted to a group of citizens, the In stitution of Santa Maria; later on, i 1258, the management was take over by the monks of San Galgan until 1314.

Already in 1215 the work was we set-up and the dome and the old aps were completed in about 1265. Lati cross plan, three aisles, hexagona dome and apse, were the essenti characteristics of the work which wa afterwards covered with marble Then began a long period of reor ganisation, demolition and enlarge ment projects. In 1284 Giovani Pisano was called to replace the fa çade with a more sumptuous one, b

didn't bring the work to a conclu-
on and when he left Siena in 1296
ıly the lower part of its masterpiece
ad been built. Soon afterwards the
orks were suspended. In the mean-
me the Sienese decided in favour of
first enlargement of the edifice, a
rolongation of the apse side, and in
317, with the work of Camaino di
rescentino, a new building site was
t up. The works had already begun
hen, in August 23 1339, the Great
ouncil of the Republic, considering
ie increase in population and the ex-
anding power of the town, decided
accomplish a more ambitious
lan: a building complex with three
isles to be built on the right side of
ie half-erected church which would
ien become the transept of the new
emple. Lando di Pietro, engineer,
culptor and goldsmith, began the
onstruction. When he died in 1340
iovanni di Agostino was entrusted
ith the work. A few years later, in
348, the works were suspended and
ien definitively abandoned, in 1355,
wing to irreparable static faults of
ie new construction and to financial
roblems weighing on the town af-
er the outbreak of pestilence and po-
tical hostilities.

The great dream was abandoned
nd attention was directed towards
he completion of the old church.
Jnder the direction of Domenico di
gostino the dangerous parts of the
bandoned complex were demoli-
hed, the vaults made higher, be-
ween 1356 and 1359 the upper part
f the façade was built by Giovanni
i Cecco, and in 1382 the apse was
ompleted. The troubled events of
his centuries old construction,
lifficulties and changes of purpose,
eft their mark on several irregular
nd asymmetrical architectural situ-
tions: in spite of this and thanks to
he remarkable work of Giovanni
Pisano the Siena Cathedral is today
considered as a masterpiece of medieval art and numbered among the most beautiful cathedrals in Italy.

The exterior. The cathedral façade is entirely built with white marble and some Sienese red and Prato green polychrome blocks: it is the most decorative element of the construction.

It is clearly subdivided into two parts and is particularly rich in movements of volumes and sculptural elements, dedicated completely to the glorification of the Virgin: the preparation for her Advent, tales drawn from the Old Testament in the lower part, the Assumption to Heaven and tales of the New Testament in the upper part. As we recounted before, the façade in the lower part is by Giovanni Pisano and it is composed of three large portals, splayed and surmounted by triangular cusps. The central arch is round while the side ones are slightly ogival. The work draws its inspiration from the Gothic style with the adorning leaves, flowers, figures and symbolic animals. In the architrave of the central portal there is a bas-relief attributed to Tino di Camaino, «The Story of San Gioacchino and Sant'Anna», and has on two of its sides sheaves of small columns with interesting classical decorations by Pisano. This same artist or his school did all the statues that, leaning from the cornices, bring plastic movement to the façade with valuable sculptural effects. The central bronze portal was made in 1958 by the sculptor Enrico Manfini: episodes of the Virgin Mary's life and the characters that have glorified her memory entirely inspired the pictures. The upper part, separated from the lower one by a cornice, is in the flowered-Gothic style, clearly drawing inspiration from the Orvieto Cathedral by Maitani. It is a work by Giovanni di Cecco, conceived with a three cusps design, showing the off-centre architecture of the central pillars in relation to the lower portal, that creates an evident discordant effect. The excellent quality of movement and the pictorical effect of the upper part is marked by the dark holes of the rose-window, the small

Full moon over the Cathedral.

loggias and the cavities on the small side towers. The cusps gables are decorated with mosaics made in 1877 by Augusto Castellani to a design by Luigi Mussini and Alessandro Franchi and they represent: in the middle, The Coronation of Mary; on the left, The Presentation; on the right, the Crib.

The central rose-window is sur rounded with thirty-four busts of Pro phets and Patriarchs of the Church In the triangles there are the fou Evangelists and, in the middle ove the rose-window, the figure of th Virgin Mary.

The originals of this work of th 14th century by Corbella, and als

he statues placed in the lower part of Giovanni Pisano's façade, have been rescued from degradation by atmospherical agents and preserved in the Museum of the Opera. The angel on the top of the central cusp is by Tommaso Redi (1639). The floor before the entrance portals is composed of marble marquetries with figures inspired by the Ceremony of Ordination. The originals (in the middle of the 15th century) are by

The Cathedral.

Nastagio di Gaspare. Over the two columns beside the platform of the Church Square are the Sienese She-wolf and the Twins, a copy of the works of Giovanni Pisano and Urbano da Cortona preserved in the Museum of the Opera.

The left side of the cathedral is incorporated into the main portion of the Archbishop's Palace and has only a closed window without mullions.

The right side is lined horizontally with the buttresses of the pillars that divide the aisle, each one of them surmounted with a statue of a Prophet (the originals date back to the 14th century). Vertically it is lined with dark marble longitudinal strips. Above each pillar there are four big tabernacle windows. The cross-vault, covered like the side and the rest of the edifice, has five big mullioned windows. In the lunette of the portal there is a marble bas-relief representing the Virgin with Child, by Donatello, that is remembered as the Forgiving Virgin. The bronze portal is a work of 1946 by Vico Consorti.

The Romanesque bell tower is inspired by Lombard-Pisan architecture. It was built in 1313 on the already existing tower of the Bisdomini-Forteguerri by Agostino di Giovanni and Agnolo di Ventura. It is decorated with white and black marble longitudinal strips: the openings are progressive, from simple windows to six mullioned windows. On the top there is an octagonal based pyramidal cusp and four smaller pyramids on the corner pillars.

The cupola has been conceived with an hexagonal plan resting on a tambour with two superimposed lines of galleries: the lower one has lancet arches between double columns, the upper one round arches. Robust ribs converge at the central lantern.

The interior. The magnificence of the work immediately strikes you as you enter the cathedral. The plan is Latin cross, the dimensions are 89 metres in length and over 24 metres in width (at the cross-vault it is 54 metres wide). The longitudinal axis goes slightly towards the right near the presbytery and this is the most evident irregularity due to the continuous adjustments required in the building. It is divided into three aisles by variously styled pillars supporting round arches and is covered with vaults, elevated during the 14th century by Camaino di Crescentino, of a light-blue colour with golden stars. The walls are covered with white and black marble strips disposed longitudinally. They enrich the interior by contrasting the vertical line and adding a particularly refined chromatic effect. In the nave and the presbytery, among the arches and the vaults, runs a continuous cornice propped up by 172 busts of popes acting as corbels. In the middle of the apse there is the bust of Christ. All these works were made between the 15th and 16th centuries. 36 busts of

1. The Bell Tower and dome seen from Jacopo della Quercia Square; 2. Nave of the Cathedral.

emperors are disposed lower down and at regular intervals. Beside the first pillars there are two classical holy water stoups made by Antonio Federighi in 1462-1463.

The floor. The floor decorations are undoubtedly one of most interesting works we find inside the Temple. There are 56 marble squares with various figures made with Graphite and inlay work in different periods between the middle of the 14th century and the middle of the 16th century. The oldest are the Graphite ones: they are engraved on marble slabs and the drills are coated with black stucco to make the drawing show up better. This is the most precious part of the works and can be seen only during a brief period of the year, from the 15th of August to the 15th of September.

In the following period the Graphite was drawn on a dark background to make the drawings show up better. The most recent ones have been made with marquetry using marbles of different colours. During the course of time they underwent several restorations and some of them have been replaced with copies (nave, No 2, 3, 5), while the other ones have been partly or entirely remade by Alessandro Franchi in 1870 (the whole area under the dome and beside on the right, Nos 16 and 17). More than 40 artists worked on this operation, mainly from Siena. Among them one can mention Domenico Beccafumi, who drew 35 paintings with Biblical subjects between 1317 and 1547; Domenico di Nicola, Pietro del Minella, Matteo di Giovanni, Bastiano di Francesco, Urbano da Cortona, Antonio Federighi, Paolo di Martino, Neroccio and the Pinturicchio. The following is a short list of the subjects and the artists of all the works according to the areas.

Nave: No 1, Hermes Trismegisto by Giovanni di Stefano (1488); No 2, Coats of Arms of Siena, in the middle, and around them those of Pisa, Lucca, Arezzo, Orvieto, Rome, Perugia, Viterbo, Massa, Volterra, Pistoia; No 3, The Imperial Eagle (1373); No 4, *The Fortune* by Paolo Mannucci based on a drawing by Pinturicchio (1504-1506); No 5, Fortune and Four Philosophers.

Left aisle: No 6, The Lybyan Sybil by Guidoccio Cozzarelli (1483); No 7, The Hellespontic Sybil by Neroccio di Bartolomeo Landi (1483); No 8, The Phrygian Sybil by Urbano da Cortona (1483); No 9, The Samyan Sybil by Matteo di Giovanni (1483); No 10, The Albunean of Tiburtinan Sybil by Benvenuto di Giovanni (1483).

Right aisle: No 11, The Delphic Sybil by Urbano da Cortona (1482); No 12, The Cumean Sybil also by Urbano da Cortona (1482); No 13, The Cumae Sybil by Giovanni di Stefano (1482); No 14, *The Eritrean Sybil* by Antonio Federighi (1482) and No 15, The Persian Sybil by Urbano da Cortona (1483).

Right transept: No 16, The Seven Ages of Man by Antonio Federighi (1475); No 17, Faith, Hope, Charity and Religion by Domenico Beccafu-

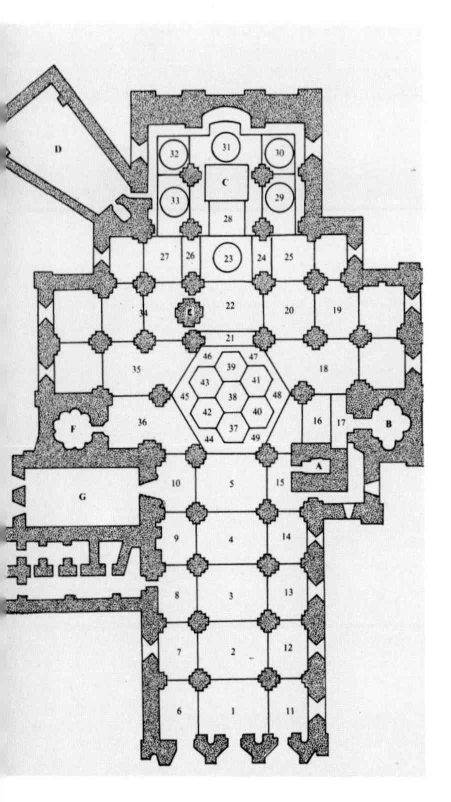

Plan of the Cathedral: Legend

Numbers correspond to the sequence followed in the main text.

A - Tomb of Bishop Tommaso Piccolomini del Testa
B - Madonna del Voto or Chigi Chapel
C - High Altar
D - Sacristy
E - Pulpit
F - Chapel S. Giovanni Battista
G - Piccolomini Library

1. Cathedral: the floor. The Slaughter of the Innocents, by Matteo di Giovanni.

mi (this and the previous work are copies remade by Alessandro Franchi in 1870); No 18, The Victory of Jefte against the Ammonites by Bastiano di Francesco (1482); No 19, The Death of Absalom by Pietro del Minella (1447) and No 20, The Emperor Siegmund on the Throne by Domenico di Bartolo (1434).

Presbytery: No 21, *Moses makes the water spring from the rock* by Domenico Beccafumi (1525); No 22, The Adoration of the Golden Calf by Domenico Beccafumi (1522); No 23, David the Psalmist, David throwing the stone and Goliath struck by it, by Domenico di Niccolò (1423); No 24, Moses by Paolo di Martino (1426); No 25, The Victory of Samson over the Philistines by Paolo di Martino (1426); No 26, The Victory of Joshua over the King of the Amohorreans by Paolo di Martino (1426); No 27, Joshua by Domenico di Niccolò (1426); No 28 *The Sacrifice of Abraham* by Domenico Beccafumi (1546); No 29, Prudence by Marchese d'Adamo (1380); No 30, Temperance by Marchese d'Adamo (1380); No 31, Mercy by Marchese d'Adamo (1380); No 32, *Justice* by Marchese d'Adamo, probably a reproduction of a drawing by Ambrogio Lorenzetti (1406) and No 33, Strength, also by Marchese d'Adamo (1406).

Left transept: No 34, Judith beheading Holophernes and the Battle on the outskirts of Betulla, by Antonio Federighi (1473); No 35, *The Slaughter of the Innocents* by Matteo di Giovanni (1481) and No 36, Hercules chased from the throne by Benvenuto di Giovanni (1484).

Area under the dome: The original works were executed by Domenico Beccafumi and Alessandro Franchi in 1870 remade them all, partly or in their entirety; No 37, Elijah ascends to Heaven; No 38, The Pact between Elijah and Ahab; No 39, The Sacrifice of Ahab; No 40, The Rebuke of Elijah; No 41, The killing of the fals Prophets; No 42, The Death of Ahab; No 43, The Sacrifice of Elijah; in the rhombuses around the previous drawings: No 44 Elijah raises from the dead the son of the widow; No 45, Elijah annoints Jehu; No 46, Ahrdia leads Ahab to Elijah; No 47, Elijah orders Ahrdia to lead him to Ahab; No 48, Elijah nourished by deers and finally No 49, Elijah asks the widow for bread.

Let us now continue the visit of the interior of the cathedral.

Internal façade. The sumptuous central portal with columns has some bas-reliefs on the pedestals. They represent the Stories of Holy Mary, a work of 1482 by Urbano da Cortona and they come from the Old Chapel of the Virgin of the Graces.

The richly decorated columns were made by Giovanni di Stefano and they come from the old altar of the Four Crowned Saints. The architrave bears the 15th century bas-reliefs representing the Stories of Sant'Ansano. The stained glass of the rose-window represents the Last Supper and was made in 1549 by Pastorino de Pastorini, based on cartoons by Perin del Vega.

Right aisle. In a niche against the façade one finds the statue of Pope Paul the Fifth made by Fulvio Signorini in 1605; at the first altar, there is a San Gaetano by Domenico Maria Canuti; at the second, The Ecstasy of San Gerolamo by Annibale Mazzuoli in 1671; at the third, the Ecstasy of San Francesco di Sales by Raffaele Vanni in 1654; and, lastly, at the fourth altar The Mystic Wedding of Santa Caterina by Pier Dandini. At the end of the aisle, after the side entrance, we find the door letting onto the bell tower. Around this door there are six scenes of Holy Mary's life painted by Urbano da Cortona, coming from the Chapel of the Graces. Over them there is the tomb of Bishop Tommaso Piccolomini del Testa, made by Neroccio in 1484-1485.

The Dome. The dome with an hexagonal plan is supported by six pillars: two poles coming from the Sienese Carroccio which took part in

Cathedral: 1. The floor; 2. Chapel of the Virgin of the Vow.

the Battle of Montaperti lean on two pillars of the nave. At every corner six columns support six large, golden statues of Saints made by Ventura Tiparilli and by Sebastiano di Francesco. The overhanging shell-shaped niches turn the hexagon of the base into a dodecagon along which runs a blind gallery subdivided by 42 architraved small columns. In the middle of each of them are figures of Patriarchs and Prophets, painted by Guidoccio Cozzarelli, Bastiano di Francesco, Benvenuto di Giovanni and Pellegrino di Mariano. The ceiling of the dome is painted with false lacunas and, above, the lantern is clearly off-centre in relation to the axis of the pillars' base.

Right transept. It is subdivided in

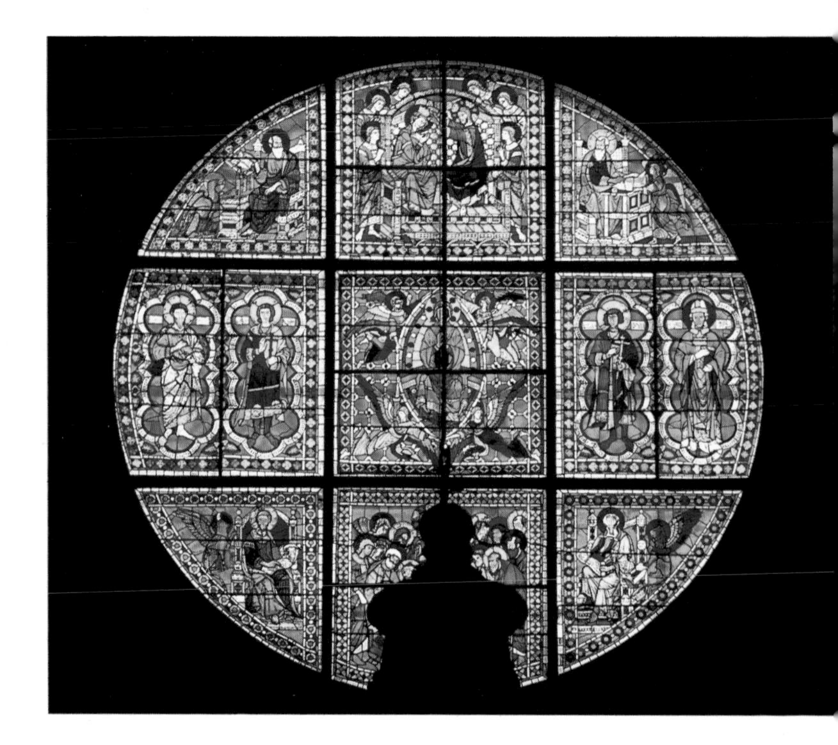

the same way as the other transept, into two aisles by pillars of different styles. On the right there is the *Chapel of the Virgin of the Vow* or Chigi, required by Pope Alexander the Seventh (Fabio Chigi from Siena), built according to a plan by Gian Lorenzo Bernini in 1661. It has a central plan, golden dome and tambour, rich in decorations, marbles and bronzes, it is a classic example of the 18th century Baroque taste. Among the works preserved in it we find: on the altar, a Virgin of the Vow, a painting from the second half of the 13th century by the School of Guido da Siena. Around it there are bronze angels by Bernini. Also the two statues placed in the entrance, San Girolamo and Santa Maria Maddalena, are by Bernini. In the niches close to the altar there is a Saint Catherine of Siena by Ercole Ferrata and a San Bernardino by Antonio Raggi, a Visitation by Carlo Maratta and a mosaic by the same author, The Flight into Egypt.

Going out of the chapel one finds, also in the transept, a statue of Alexander the Seventh, on the right of the first altar, by Antonio Raggi (1663); in front of it there is a statue of Alexander the Seventh by Ercole Ferrata (1668); on the altar there is a San Bernardino Preaching by Mattia Preti (1650) and a San Crescenzio by Luigi Mussini (1867).

Continuing there is the Chapel of the Sacrament: on the walls there are five bas-reliefs representing the four Evangelists by Giovanni di Francesco from Imola and, in the middle, a Saint Paul by Giovanni di Turino made in 1425; on the altar there is the Adoration of the Shepherds by Alessandro Casolani (1594).

Cathedral: 1. Stained-glass window in the apse representing the Death, Assumption and Coronation of the Virgin. The Four Evangelists and the Four Patron Saints of Siena; 2. Pensile basin, masterpiece of goldsmithery by Giovanni di Turino; 3. Saint Bernardino preaching in Piazza del Campo, work by Sano di Pietro.

2

3

Presbytery. In the middle of the presbytery there is the main altar, a marble work by Baldassarre Peruzzi (1532). Over it there is a big bronze ciborium by Vecchietta (1467-1472) coming from the church of the Santa Maria della Scala Hospital and placed there, in 1506, to replace a Majesty by Duccio preserved in the Museum of the Opera. The two candelstick-angels up above are by Giovanni di Stefano (1489), the lower ones are real masterpieces by Francesco di Giorgio Martini made between 1497 and 1499.

Eight bronze angels made by Domenico Beccafumi (1548-1550) can be seen on the columns. Up above, one facing the other, there are two chancels: the one on the right was made by Antonio Barili (1511). The left one (1550) was designed by Riccio as was the Bishop's seat (made in the first years of the 20th century). There is also a residence lectern and the lectern behind the altar.

Apse. In the niche of the apse there were frescoes by Beccafumi of which the following are left, restored and mainly repainted in 1817: The Paradise and the Apostles (1544); further down, an Assumption by Bartolomeo Cesi (1594); at the sides, fresco works by Ventura Salimbeni, Esther and Assuero on the right, The Jews in the Desert on the left and, at the extreme edges, figures of Saints. The precious circular stained-glass window is the oldest work of this kind in Italy: it represents the Death, Assumption and Coronation of the Virgin, the four Evangelists and the four Patron Saints of Siena. It is a work by Duccio di Buoninsegna (1288) made on cartoons. The wonderful wooden choir runs all around. The work was begun in 1363 and finished in 1397. Originally there were 90 stalls, in two rows, with baldachins and tabernacles of Saints, made by Francesco and Giacomo del Tonghio. Only the parts at the side of the niche remain.

In 1503 the remarkable inlaid mirrors made by the friar Giovanni da Verona were added to the choir. They were originally designed for the choir of the Monastery of San Benedetto outside the Tufi gate, while the central stalls designed by

Riccio and built by Teseo di Bartolino and Benedetto di Giovanni, date back to the second half of the 16th century.

Chapter House. We enter the Sacristy from the door on the left of the apse. This door is adorned with a golden bronze hanging pileus, white marble and enamel, a refined goldsmith's masterpiece by Giovanni di Turino (1437). From here, through a vestibule in which we can see a bronze bust of Alexander the Seventh made by Melchiorre Caffa, disciple of Bernini, we enter the Chapter House. This is adorned with portraits of Sienese Bishops and Popes. Moreover, on the far wall, there is a Virgin with Child and the Saints Sebastiano and Rocco, attributed to Giacomo Pacchiarotti, having at the two sides two small paintings by Sano di Pietro, Saint Bernardino preaching in the Square of the Campo (1430) and in San Francesco Square (1440). It is interesting to notice in these paintings the architecture of Palaces in the 15th century. On the left wall there is a San Bernardino also by Sano di Pietro (1470).

Left transept. Coming back to the transept, on the left, beside the dome pillars, there is the splendid *pulpit* sculpted by the master Nicola Pisano between 1266 and 1268, with the help of his son Giovanni and his disciples Arnolfo di Cambio, Donato and Lapo di Ricevuto. This splendid construction, similar to and slightly more recent than the hexagonal pulpit of the Pisa Cathedral, represents an important stylistic evolution for Gothic Italian sculpture. Comparing this work with the one in Pisa we feel that all Byzantine rigidity and solemnity is over, while expressive power and plastic harmony gain advantage.

The pulpit, on an octagonal plan, is held up by nine columns of green marble, granite and porphyry. Four of these columns are without bases, four are supported by lions and lionesses tearing other animals to pieces and the central one rests on a sculpted base on which the eight liberal arts

Cathedral: 1. Pulpit, sculpted between 1266 and 1269 by Nicola Pisano; 2. Monument to the Cardinal Riccardo Petroni, work by Tino di Camaino; 3. Tombstone in bronze belonging to the Bishop Giovanni Pecci, made by Donatello in 1426.

are represented: Grammar, Dialectics, Rhetoric, Philosophy, Arithmetic, Geometry, Astronomy and Music.

The Corinthian capitals of the columns are linked with elegant trilobed arches, with figures of Prophets on the pendentives, while above the capitals statues of the Virtues keep the arches separated. The parapet is composed of seven basreliefs, one for each side, separated by figures of Prophets and angels and the Seven Stories of Christ are represented: Nativity and Visitation; Arrival and Adoration of the Magi; Presentation in the Temple; the Dream of Joseph and Flight to Egypt; Slaughter of the Innocents; Crucifixion; and Final Judgement of Wicked and Final Judgement of the Good People. On the eighth side rises up the richly decorated stairway remade on a design of Riccio.

Coming back to visit the transept on the right we find the chapel of Sant'Ansano in a corner. In it we find: on the altar Sant'Ansano baptising the Sienese by Francesco Vanni (1596); on the left side the monument to the Cardinal Riccardo Petroni, built by Tino di Camaino (1317-18). The Sarcophagus in basrelief is propped up by four caryatid angels on corbels. Over the lying figure with four angels there is a tabernacle with the figure of the Virgin with Child and, at its sides, Saint Peter and Saint Paul. On the floor of the chapel there is a bronze tomb slab of the Bishop Giovanni Pecci, made by Donatello in 1426. Following on out of the chapel there is a statue of Pius the Second seated, by Giuseppe Mazzuoli (1698) and, on the floor, a Graphite tomb stone (1468). At the first altar we find a painting representing the Virgin, the Saints Peter and Paul, by Salvatore Fontana finished by Raffaele Vanni; at the second altar a 14th century wooden crucifix and a statue of the Virgin, John the Evangelist and Mary Magdalene of the 17th century. On the left we find a statue by Pietro Balestra (1706) representing the Pope Pius the Third.

One enters then the *Chapel of San Giovanni Battista*. It is designed symmetrically and with the same plan of

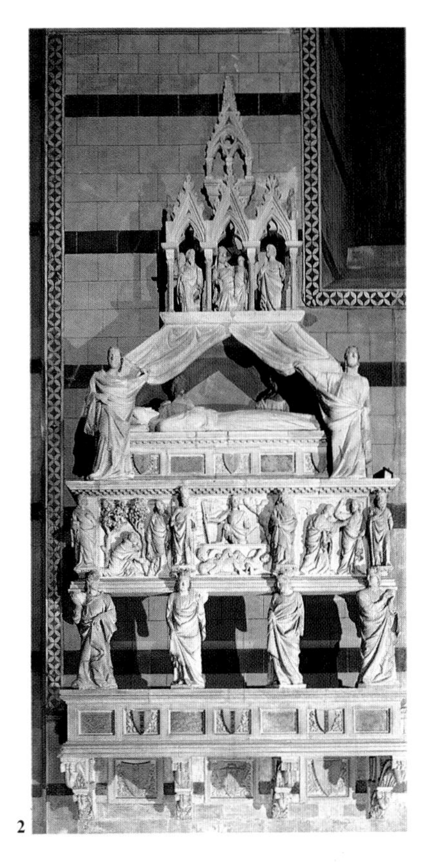

2

3

1

the chapel of the Virgin of the Vow. We enter it through a marble portal by Marrina whose base columns are attributed to Federighi. The iron gate is by Gallustio Barili. The chapel is a Renaissance construction by Giovanni di Stefano (1482). It it richly decorated with stuccoes by Alberto Caponeri and Cosimo Lucchi (1596) and holds several works of art: from the left a Pinturicchio fresco (1504), a portrait of young Alberto Aringhieri; a statue of Sant'Ansano by Giovanni di Stefano (1487); a Nativity of the Baptist by Pinturicchio (1504); a famous bronze statue of the Baptist, a late work by Donatello, dated 1457; The Decapitation of the Baptist by Pinturicchio but remade by Rustichino in 1608; a statue of Saint Catherine of Alexandria (1487) by Neroccio and finished by other artists; a portrait of old Alberto Aringhieri by Pinturicchio; above, a Baptist in the Desert, also by Pinturicchio; a Baptism of Jesus by Rustici; Saint John Preaching, by Pinturicchio; Saint John in prison by Cesare Maccari.

The marble font, placed in the middle of the chapel, is by Antonio Federighi who made it after 1484. It bears eight sculptured sides: six stories of Adam and Eve, Samson and the Lion, and Hercules and the Centaur.

Going out of the chapel we find on the right the monument to Marcantonio Zonzadari, made by Giuseppe and Bartolomeo Mazzuoli in 1725.

Left aisle. In the first sector there is the monumental marble façade of the *Piccolomini Library*. It was commissioned by Cardinal Francesco Todeschini Piccolomini, afterwards elected to the Papal throne with the name of Pius the Third. He wanted to preserve the library of his uncle from his mother's side, the Pope Pius the Second. The façade is architecturally based on two arcades decorated by Marrina (1487). Inside the right arch there is a small altar with a bas-relief representing Saint John the Evangelist by Giovanni di Stefano: below the altar a Pietà, a wooden group by Alberto di Betto. Inside the left arch there is the entrance door of the Library. Over the door, in a big

Cathedral: 1. Chapel of Saint John the Baptist; 2. Bronze statue of the Baptist, work by Donatello dated in 1457; 3. Interior of the Piccolomini Library, and the famous group of the Three Graces.

lunette, is represented the Coronation of Pius the Third, a fresco by Pinturicchio.

The inside of the Library is a single great hall completely covered with frescoes by Pinturicchio painted between 1502 and 1509. In the middle, on a Renaissance style base, there is the renowned Group of the Three Graces: it is a Roman copy dating back to the 3rd century A.D., reproducing, very probably, a Greek painting of the Hellenistic age: the work was donated so that it would be displayed in the Library, by Cardinal Francesco Todeschini Piccolomini himself. On the vault, subdivided into squares, one finds mythological and allegorical objects: in the centre is the Piccolomini Family's coat of arms surrounded with fruit shoots. On the walls there are 10 panels frescoed with rare brightness and grace. They are subdivided by pilaster strips and crowned with pendentives decorated with extremely beautiful grotesque paintings. The 10 panels represent scenes of the life of Pius the Second, Enea Silvio Piccolomini, renowned personage of humanist cul-

1

ture, born in Corsignana, near Pienza, in 1405, Arcbishop of Siena from 1450 to 1458, then Pope from 1458 to 1464.

The squares represent, beginning from the window at the bottom on the right: Piccolomini's departure towards the Basilea Council; ambassador of the Council to King James of Scotland; Poet Laureate by the Emperor Frederick the Third; sent as an envoy by Frederick the Third to Pope Eugenio the Fourth; as Bishop of Siena he introduces, near Camollia Gate, Eleonora of Portugal to her fiancé, Frederick the Third; his election to Cardinal by Pope Callisto the Third; the ascending to the papal throne; as Pope Pius the Second he supports the crusade against the Turks in Mantova; the proclamation of the canonization of Catherine of Siena and lastly Pius the Second going to Ancona to hasten the departure of the crusade. Below the frescoes, on a series of wooden benches inlaid by Antonio Barili in 1469, splendid books of anthems are displayed. They are the property of the Cathedral and of the Hospital of Santa Maria della Scala, illuminated by the following masters: Liberale da Verona, Girolamo da Verona, Sano di Pietro, Pellegrino di Mariano and Guidoccio Cozzarelli. Above the entrance is placed a bas-relief, representing the expulsion of Adam and Eve from Paradise, a copy of the works of the Gaia Fountain. Some

people think Jacopo della Quercia did it himself. Between the windows there is a bronze statue of the Resurrected Christ, made by Fulvio Signorini in 1595. The majolica floor is decorated with the same coats of arms of the Piccolomini Family. Going out of the Piccolomini Library and continuing the visit of the left aisle we find a monument to Bandino Bandini with a sculpture representing the Resurrected Christ among two angels of Michelangelo's School (second half of the 16th century): then the Piccolomini altar, a remarkable work by Andrea Bregno in 1503.

Cathedral: Piccolomini Library; 1. Illuminated anthem book. Peter and Andrew leave their nets to follow Christ; 2. Pinturicchio: Piccolomini, dressed as the Bishop of Siena, presents, at the Gate Camollia, Eleonora of Portugal to her fiancé Frederick III; 3. Pinturicchio: Piccolomini, appointed poet laureate by the Emperor Frederick III.

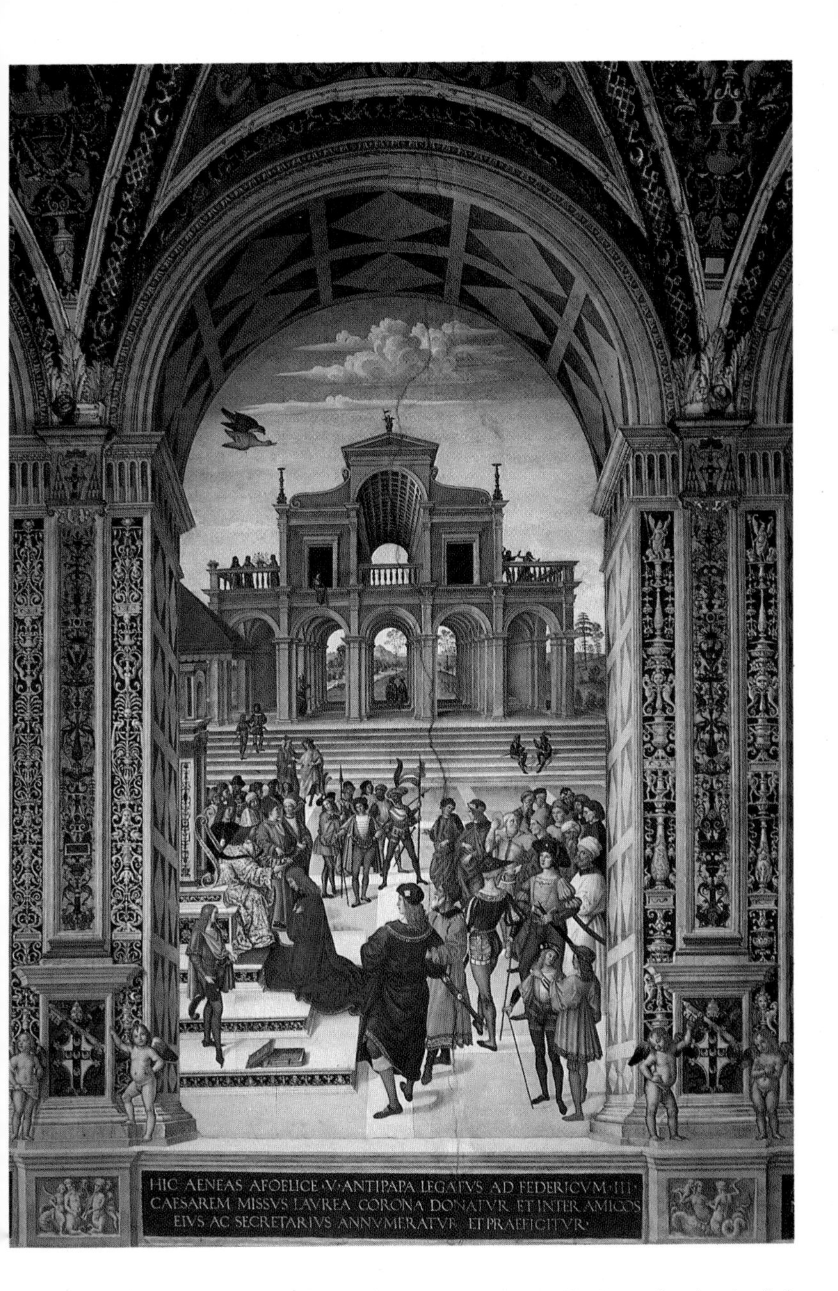

HIC AENEAS A FOELICE V ANTIPAPA LEGATVS AD FEDERICVM III
CAESAREM MISSVS LAVREA CORONA DONATVR ET INTER AMICOS
EIVS AC SECRETARIVS ANNVMERATVR ET PRAEFICITVR

The statues in the niches, around the altar, of Saint Gregory and Saint Paul, on the right, and Saint Peter and Saint Pius, on the left, are early works by Michelangelo (1501-1504), who later on completed the San Francesco, which is placed above on the left, and which Torreggiani had begun. The Virgin, placed above on the left, is considered to be an early work by Jacopo della Quercia. At the following altars there are: an Epiphany by Pietro Sorri (1588), a Christ with San Giacomo and San Filippo by Francesco Trevisani (1688) and the Four Crowned Saints by the same author.

THE NEW CATHEDRAL

Walking along the right side of the Cathedral one comes to the massive remains of the New Cathedral. The enlargement of the Cathedral, which should have occupied the entire surface of Jacopo della Quercia square, would have transformed, as has been mentioned before, the present cathedral into the transept of the larger project. Works began in 1339, under the leadership of Lando di Pietro and, later, of Giovanni and Domenico di Agostino, and were definitely interrupted in 1355. The only structures remaining of the Cathedral are the right aisle, with five arches, the façade with a large window divided longitudinally in two parts, a portion of the left wall with three large arches and windows. The building of the Prefettura nowadays rests on this left hand wall. If these 54 meters of the structure had been added, the new temple would have reached massive proportions (over 109 metres). The monument, taking into account the refined architecture and decoration, would have gained an admirably high artistic value.

MUSEUM OF THE METROPOLITAN INSTITUTION

The first three closed arcades of the right aisle of the New Cathedral house the Museum of the Metropolitan Institution. It was established in 1870 and since then it has been renewed and enriched many times. The collection is mainly composed of works coming from the Cathedral either to ensure their good preservation or because they have simply been moved into the Museum from the Cathedral. It is a collection of sculptures, paintings, bronzes, earthenware, wooden and goldsmith's works, embroidery and very artistically valuable miniatures. The fame of all these works is tied in above all with the Sienese and Tuscan school masterpieces of the 13th, 14th and 15th centuries by Giovanni Pisano, Duccio di Buoninsegna, Simone Martini, Pietro Lorenzetti and Jacopo della Quercia.

Ground floor. On the ground floor one enters a large hall divided in two parts by a wrought iron railing of the 15th century which rests on marble plutei from the school of Nicola Pisano: in this hall one finds sculptures and architectural pieces coming mainly from the interior of the Cathedral.

1. Panoramic view with, in the foreground, the façade of the New Cathedral; 2. Museum of the Cathedral: Hall of Giovanni Pisano; 3. Hall of Giovanni Pisano. Jacopo della Quercia, Virgin with Child, Saint Girolamo and offerer.

In the first room one can find: on he left wall haut-reliefs representing he Annunciation, the Nativity, the light to Egypt and the Epiphany end of the 13th century), coming rom the parish Church of Ponte allo pino; the front of a Roman sar-ophagus with sea gods (Imperial ge); a marble pluteus with the later Ecclesiae and the Symbols of he Four Evangelists, by Lapo of iovanni Pisano's School; a bas-elief, Saint Bernardino by Urbano a Cortona; a statue of Saint Peter, y the same author; a Lion, by iovanni Pisano.

3

In the second room one can find: oon after the railing, the originals of he two she-wolves once placed on he columns before the Cathedral, ne by Giovanni Pisano, the other by iovanni da Cortona. In the centre of the hall there is a beautiful haut-elief, the Virgin with Child, San irolamo and the Cardinal Casini on is knees, by Jacopo della Quercia. he work was once placed in the athedral, on the altar of Cardinal asini, and then disappeared for a ong time, but now it is again in Sie-a; on the floor a tombal slab by ommaso Pecci of the 14th century and several fragments coming from he Cathedral floor. Three of them efer to the Sacerdotal Ordination, and are works by Nastagio de Gaspa-re (1450); six hexagons representing the Ages of Man by Antonio Federi-ghi (1475), and six Biblical Episodes by Beccafumi. Beside the pillars there are ten statues, masterpiece sculp-tured for the Cathedral façade by Giovanni Pisano between 1284 and 1286. They are a very effective exam-ple of Gothic sculpture in Europe; from left to right are represented Moses, Mary of Moses, Simeon, a Sybil, Isaiah, Balaam, David, Abacuc, Plato and Solomon. Some sculptures by the School of Pisano are placed every two pillars. Some of them have the mark of Pisano's hand. Along the left wall: fragments by Giovanni di Cecco of the second half of the 14th century, represent-ing the Holy Virgin with Child and Christ's ancestor, coming from the rose-window of the Cathedral fa-

çade; two Bulls and a Horse by Giovanni Pisano. On the bottom wall the Baptism of Christ, a great altarpiece by Brescianino (1524) inside an altar of 1689.

First floor. Going up to the first floor one enters into the so-called *hall of Duccio*, which houses the very famous «Majesty» painted between 1308 and 1311 by Duccio di Buonin-

egna, placed on the Cathedral's main altar until 1505. Thanks to this masterpiece the painter became the leading master of the Sienese pictorial school. This work fuses admirably the inspiration of the Byzantine art with the lyricism of French-oriented Gothic art.

The large wooden altar-piece, painted on both sides, was sawed in 1771 to make it more visible to people and was moved to the Museum of the Institution in 1878. On one side many figures are represented: the Virgin with Child on the Throne among Angels, Saints Peter, John the Baptist, Agnese, Paul, John the Evangelist, Agata, and the four patron saints of the town, Ansano, Savino, Crescenzio and Vittore; above, bust of the Ten Apostles are decoratively represented.

At the base of the throne one can see a Latin writing which means «Holy Mother of God, bring about peace for Siena, give new life to Duccio because hereby he painted You». The back of the painting is opposite the «Majesty»: it is composed of 20 partitions with episodes of Christ's Passion ordered from left to right and from high to low; Entry into Jerusalem, the Washing of the Feet and the Last Supper; the Pact of Judas and the Oration in the Garden; Christ before Anne and the Denial of Peter; Christ beaten and Christ before Caifa; Christ Charged by the Pharisees and Christ before Pilate; above Christ Taken back to Pilate and Christ before Herod; the Flagellation and the Crown of thorns; Going to Calvary and Pilate Washing his Hands; the Crucifixion; Deposition in the Tomb and Deposition of the Cross; Mary at the Tomb and the Descent towards Limbo; the Apparition in Emmaus and «Noli me Tangere». Other paintings also belonged to the altar-piece of the «Majesty». They are partly lost and partly preserved elsewhere: in the Museum we find only 19 small boards belonging to the predella and to the altar-piece. The same hall houses a triptych with the Nativity of the Virgin, signed and dated in 1342 by the artist Pietro Lorenzetti, a real master-

1. Museum of the Cathedral. Hall of Duccio, the Majesty (front); 2. The Majesty (back). Masterpiece by Duccio di Buoninsegna painted between 1308 and 1311.

MATER SCA DEI
SIS CAUSA SENIS REQUIEI SIS DUCIO VITA TE QUIA
PINXIT ITA

piece of his artistic maturity, and a Virgin Mary with Child, an early work by Duccio, coming from the Church of Santa Cecilia in Crevole. Through a door on the right one enters a room three quarters of which have pieces of furniture designed by Riccio in the 16th century, and from here one enters a hall in which are preserved eight illuminated codes, coming from the Cathedral and from the Hospital of Santa Maria della Scala (15th and 16th centuries); documents concerning the artists who worked in the Cathedral; architectural drawings and projects. Coming back to Duccio's hall, through a door on the left one enters a hall with mullioned windows which belonged to the construction of the New Cathedral. In this hall several 19th century cartoons for the Cathedral floor are exposed together with the sketches for the façade mosaics and several 14th and 15th centuries books of anthems.

Treasure Hall. Between the first and the second floor we can enter the Treasure Hall which houses the most precious vestments and vessels of the Cathedral and other art works. We notice a Reliquiary of San Galgano's head, coming from the Abbey dedicated to the Saint (13th century); a Reliquiary of San Clemente of the 17th century; a silk frontal embroidered in gold and silver of the 16th century; a terracotta statue of Saint John the Evangelist by Giacomo Cozzarelli; the Crown of San Galgano of the end of the 13th century; a golden rose, a gift by Alessandro the Seventh in 1658; a sketch by Bernini for a painting of San Girolamo; a small wooden Crucifix by Giovanni Pisano having at its side the images of the Holy Virgin and Saint John the Evangelist made by Giovanni di Paolo; wooden polychrome busts of San Crescenzio, San Vittore and San Savino by Francesco di Valdambrino of 1409; a Complaint of the Dead Christ, by Vecchietta; Christ bearing the Cross by Beccafumi and a Virgin with Child attributed to Benvenuto di Giovanni.

Museum of the Cathedral: 1. Hall of Duccio, the Majesty, Virgin with Child on the Throne (detail); 2. Virgin with Child, called the Virgin with the big eyes. Sienese painter of the beginning of the 19th century.

2

Second floor. Here one enters, in front of the entrance, the hall called of the «Virgin with the Big Eyes», the name of which derives from the painted board placed in the centre of the hall. It represents a Virgin with Child, made in relief in the first half of the 13th century: in front of this painting, the Sienese vowed to the Virgin Mary at the Battle of Montaperti. On the walls: four Saints, side partitions of a polyptych, a work by Ambrogio Lorenzetti; Articles of Credo, nine small painted boards by Nicola di Naldo; a San Girolamo by Giovanni di Paolo; the Blessed Soul Agostino Novello inspired by an angel, and four of his miracles, a masterpiece of the first half of the 14th century by Simone Martini; furniture of the end of the 14th century with stories of the Cross and busts of angels; a Virgin with Child by Sassetta; an Apparition of Saint Francis at the Chapter of Arles, a small painting by Giovanni di Paolo; a «Virgin of Milk and Saints», polyptych by Gregorio di Cecco; a

Crucifixion of the beginning of the 15th century; a Virgin Mary with Child, Angels and Saints Apollonia and Bernardino, a work by Sano di Pietro; a Virgin with Child by the Master of Città di Castello, Duccio's disciple.

Coming back to the landing, on the left one finds one's way to the *small hall of the Conversari*, famous for the lectures Vittorio Alfieri held here in 1777. It is interesting to notice among the things preserved in this hall, these works: a Saint Anthony of Padua attributed to Matteo Balducci; a Virgin Mary on the Throne among Saints John the Evangelist, Nicholas, Gregory and Girolamo. The stories of these characters are represented in the predella, by Matteo di Giovanni (1478); Holy Virgin on the Throne between Saint Anthony of Padua and Saint Bernardino by the same author, signed and dated 1460; a Saint Paul by Beccafumi (1515-1516); a Virgin Mary with Child between Saint Anthony Abbot and Sant'Agata, by Cristoforo Roncalli, called Pomarancio (1576); a Deposition and Christ before Pilate by Luca Giordano; a Holy Family attributed to Riccio and a Transfiguration of Jesus by Girolamo Genga. Numerous altar frontals are kept below the paintings. In the next room there is a rich tapestry coming from the former Monastery of Campansi and frocks and chasubles of different ages. By a winding staircase one can reach the top of the New Cathedral façade (the Large Façade) from which one can enjoy a wonderful view of the Cathedral bell-tower and dome.

THE CRYPT OF THE CATHEDRAL

The high door on the right side, among the arcades of the New Cathedral (Duomo Nuovo), faces the flight of steps leading to San Giovanni Square, called «Shore of the death», and planned by Giovanni Sabatelli in 1451.

Along the flight of steps there is the access to some rooms in the ancient crypt of the Cathedral, that recent restorations have now made visitable. In the entrance room is placed a group of statues representing the Apostles, copies of those ones already set on the New Cathedral cornices, preserved today in the Brompton Oratory in London, works of artists of the Giovanni Pisano's School. Inside the crypt, at the floor below, there is a room decorated with

3

aluable fragments of frescoes, dat-
ıg back to 1270-1280, representing
he history of the Passion of Christ,
he Madonna and the Saints. These
rescoes are some of the most ancient
xecution in existence, evidence of
he origins of the Sienese pictorial
chool. In this same room is also
reserved the statuesque group
epresenting the Redeemer between
wo genuflected angels recently re-
tored and ascribed to Giovanni di
Agostino, once set on the wonderful
ortal of the façade of the New
Cathedral and then replaced by co-
ies for a better maintenance.

BAPTISTRY

One descends again between the
New Cathedral arcades and crosses
he high door opened on the side of
he New Cathedral. Through the
teps planned by Giovanni Sabatelli
n 1451 one reaches San Giovanni
square. In this square rises the Bap-

1. Interior view of the Crypt; 2. The Redeemer, detail of the recently restored group of statues previously situated in the splendid portal of the New Cathedral; 3. Portal of the New Cathedral and stairs which lead to the Baptistery; 4. Façade of the Baptistery.

4

tistry or Pieve of San Giovanni.

The building, which is almost the crypt of the Cathedral, serves as a base for the prolongation of the Cathedral apse. It was built between 1316 and 1325. Its façade, completed in 1382, is sometimes attributed to Giacomo di Mino del Pellicciaio but it is probably a work by Domenico d'Agostino. The façade, not completed in the higher portion, is made completely of white marble which covers the Cathedral apse as well as the Baptistry. In the lower part there are three large portals; the central

one is overhung by a cusp; also, between pillars and small columns, there is a first line of small arches with a delicate design and, above it, three high and narrow blind ogival arch windows complete the architecture.

On the floor before the portals we can see worn Graphite which represents the sacraments of Baptism and Confirmation; the left one was paint-ed by Bartolomeo di Mariano, i 1450, while the others were made ac-cording to the drawings by Federigh in 1451. The rectangular interior i subdivided into three aisles by tw pillars which support the coverin vaults; it was completed in 1325 b Camaino da Crescentino and Tino d Camaino. In the centre one can ad

ıire the famous *Baptism Font* by acopo della Quercia, masterpiece of 5th century art, intermediary between Gothic and Renaissance style, ıade in the first half of the 15th century. Placed on two steps, it was ıade by Pietro del Minella, Bastiano i Corso and Nanni di Lucca as egards the architectural part, while he sculptures are by different artists. t is composed of an hexagonal bain with an hexagonal ciborium in the ıiddle supported by a pillar. On the op of the ciborium, designed by acopo della Quercia, there is a tatue of Saint John the Baptist by he same artist. Among the pediments there are four bronze angels: two of them are by Donatello and two by Giovanni di Turino (1424); in the niches there are five figures of Prophets sculptured by Jacopo della Quercia and a Virgin Mary with Child by Giovanni di Turino. Around the basin there are six bronze basreliefs with subjects of the Baptist's life separated by six statues. Going towards the right and starting from the altar side one recognizes: Zacharias chased out of the Temple, by Jacopo della Quercia (1417); the statue of Justice, by Giovanni di Turino (1424); the Birth of the Baptist by Turino di Sano (1427); Charity by Giovanni di Turino (1424); the Baptist Preaching, by the same artist (1427); Prudence, also by Giovanni di Turino; the Baptism of Jesus, by Lorenzo Ghilberti (1427); Faith, by Donatello (1428); the Capture of the Baptist, by Lorenzo Ghilberti (1427); Hope, by Donatello (1428); Herod's Banquet, by the same artist (1427);

'. Interior of the Baptistery with baptismal 'ont; 2. Baptismal font. The banquet of Ierod, by Donatello.

1

2

Strength, by Goro di Neroccio (1428).

The vault frescoes next to the façade and below the arches, represent the Apostles, Prophets and Sybils and were painted by Vecchietta in 1450; on the other vaults the Articles of Credo by Vecchietta's School (1447), on the right lunette, Jesus in the Pharisee's House, of doubtful attribution. The apse frescoes represent Jesus' life. The higher ones were painted by Michele di Matteo from Bologna and the ones below by Vecchietta (1435); on the left lunette, Miracles of Saint Anthony, attributed to Benvenuto di Giovanni (second half of the 15th century). In a niche in the left wall there is a wooden statue by Jacopo della Quercia's School.

HOSPITAL OF SANTA MARIA DELLA SCALA

Coming back to the Cathedral Square, on the left we go past the Palace of the Prefettura, of the Duke's Palace, started in 1489 according to a project by Giacomo Petrucci and completed a century later, by Bernardo Bontempi for the Medici Family, who elected it as the seat of their Governorship. If one carries on, one reaches, in front of the Cathedral, the huge complex of the Spedale di Santa Maria della Scala (Santa Maria of the Steps). It name is due to the position in whic it is placed: in front of the Cathedra

Baptistery: 1. «Strength», by Goro di Se Neroccio; 2. «Justice», by Giovanni di Tu rino; 3. «Hope», by Donatello; 4. 5. Scene of the Life of Christ: the «Scourging» an the «Walk to the Calvary».

steps. Tradition wants it that it was built in the year 832 by the Blessed Soul Sorore, a shoe-maker, while the present shape is due to the Canonicals of the Cathedral who built it between the 13th and 14th centuries. It has a long brickwork and ashlar façade, with large mullioned windows. The visit begins in the first entrance hall, the ceiling of which was decorated by Guidaccio d'Andrea (second half of the 15th century). It houses the tomb of Jacopo Tondi, a work probably by Giacomo Cozzarelli (1507). In the second hall we see a fresco of Beccafumi, the Meeting of San Gioacchino and Saint Anne, painted around 1514. In the next

room there are figures of saints, painted by Cristoforo di Bindoccio and Meo di Pietro, disciples of Lorenzetti (1370).

One enters then the large *hall of the Infirmary* or *Pellegrinaio*, the architectural rhythm of which is given by large arches and the walls of which have 15th century frescoes dedicated to the hospital mission. Most of the works are by Domenico di Bartolo (1440-1443). The frescoes are particularly interesting, being so far the only cycle of that kind, full of details of costumes and architectural views. On the vaults there are Patriarchs and Saints of the first half of the 15th century. Following on there is the infirmary of San Pio with a fresco representing the Blessed Soul Sorore in ecstasy, by Domenico di Bartolo and the hall of Saint Peter covered with Vecchietta's badly damaged frescoes of 1448. One goes back to the first hall and enters the *Church of Santa Maria della Scala* or of the Santissima Annunziata. It was built in 1252 and renewed in 1466 by Guidoccio d'Andrea; it has a single nave, an elevated presbytery, a large apse and a painted lacunar ceiling. We notice also two inlaid organs by Ventura di Sir Giuliano Turapilli, artist also of the wooden choir placed in the apse; a bronze statue represents the Resurrected Christ, made by Vecchietta in 1476; in the apse basin there is a fresco by Sebastiano Conca of 1732 representing the *Piscina Probatica*. In the sacristy a very valuable treasure is preserved: it consists of precious goldsmith's wares dated from the 10th to the 16th centuries and pieces of pottery from 14th to 16th centuries. Again through the first hall we enter the Hall of the Sick People, with painted Stories of Mary by Giuseppe Nasini and, at the altar, a Virgin Mary by Paolo di Giovanni Fei. Going down the Hospital vault we find the Oratory of Saint Catherine of Night, with a wooden 15th century choir and a marble Virgin Mary on the altar (14th century); the Sacristy, with a triptych by Taddeo di Bartolo, which dates to the begin-

1. Hospital of Santa Maria della Scala; 2. Piazza Duomo and Archbishop's Palace.

ning of the 15th century, representing the Virgin Mary with Child and Saint John the Baptist and Saint Andrew. Next to it there is the oratory of the Brotherhood of Disciplinati, now Society of the Executors of Pious Dispositions. Here we find: at the main altar, a Virgin Mary between Saint Peter and Saint Paul, by Alessandro Casolani; a Crucifix and two statues, Saint Catherine and Saint Bernardino, wooden 16th century works; in the sacristy a Final Judgement by Martino di Bartolomeo, a Saint John the Baptist by Giovanni di Paolo and a Pietà by Sano di Pietro.

ARCHBISHOP'S PALACE

Again in the Cathedral Square, on the side of it is the Archbishop's Palace. It was built between 1718 and 1728 imitating the 14th century Gothic style, trying to find an agreement with the Cathedral style. The façade is covered with white and black longitudinal strips of marble in the lower part, with brickwork in the upper part.

We can visit, in the inside, the Chapel of San Biagio, by Riccio and the Virgin of Milk, a painting on cuspidate board of high artistic value by Ambrogio Lorenzetti.

SAN SEBASTIANO IN VALLE PIATTA

Taking, on the left of the Archbishop's Palace, Fusari Street and San Girolamo Lane, one arrives into a small square, seat of the Church of San Sebastiano in Valle Piatta, oratory of the Contrada of the Wood. The brickwork construction was erected in the beginning of the 16th century by Girolamo Ponsi. It has a cylindrical dome and a sail belltower, Greek plan and decorations by 16th and 17th century Sienese artists.

TOUR OF THE TOWN NO. THREE

3

National Picture Gallery • House of Pia • Church S. Pietro alle Scale • Via Stalloreggi • Church S. Niccolò al Carmine • Church Ss. Pietro e Paolo • Chapel of the Prison of Sant'Ansano • Church Sant'Agostino • Via P.A. Mattioli • Church S. Giuseppe • Church S. Girolamo • Church S. Maria dei Servi • Oratory Ss. Trinità • Via Roma • Church S. Spirito • Church S. Martino

NATIONAL PICTURE GALLERY

Walking from Postierla Square, at the bottom of the Città Street, along San Pietro Street one reaches No 29, the *Buonsignori Palace*. It is one of the most elegant Sienese palaces of late Gothic style. It was built in the first half of the 15th century for the banker Giovanni di Guccio Bichi. It was sold a few years later to the Tagliacci brothers after which it became a property, in 1476, of the Buonsignori Family who donated it to the town so that it would become a museum site. The Palace façade is entirely of brickwork: on the ground floor there is a seat skirting board: on each floor the architectural rhythm is rendered by ogival arches and there are two lines of twice-mullioned windows separated by cornices of hanging arches. On the top the cornice is embattled. Today the Palace is the seat of the *National Picture Gallery* which has a collection of works rich in the most important Sienese masters from the 12th to the first half of the 17th centuries. It is a fundamental place for the visitors to enhance their knowledge of the Sienese pictorial school. The Abbot Giuseppe Ciaccheri began the collection at the end of the 18th century; the collection was composed from works coming from the supression of churches, convents and religious and laic confraternities, and was enriched with legacies, deposits and purchases. At the beginning of its existence the Collection was found in the Institute of Fine Arts. Under the Administration of the State in 1930 it was moved to its definitive seat at the Buonsignori Palace. There are about 700 paintings, exhibited in chronological order and stylistic affinity, in 38 halls. Greatly renowned masterpieces stand beside less important works, in a priceless assemblage that offers an artistic experience of fundamental importance. From the foyer, in which there are ancient Roman works, one enters the colonnade yard on whose walls are exhibited the 14th century sculptures and coats of arms: on the left there is a remarkable marble portal, a Renaissance work coming from the destroyed Olivetano Monastery outside the Tufi Gate, and six bas-reliefs on the wall at the far end, attributed to Giovanni di Turino, and representing the Evangelists, San Paolo and Moses: on the right one enters the Hall of Cartoons, in which there are nine cartoons with biblical scenes, made for the Cathedral by Domenico Beccafumi and, moreover, there are bronze bracelets by Giacomo Cozzarelli, a canvas by Pietro da Cortona depicting the Martyrdom of Santa Martina, a sketch by Vecchietta for the bronze ciborium placed on

1

the main altar of the Cathedral. From the foyer we ascend to the second floor. The visit to the Gallery begins here. The most important works will be pointed out hall by hall.

HALL I: the frontal representing the Redeemer and the symbols of the Evangelists and, in six side partitions, three stories of the Cross and three stories of a saint, probably Saint Helen, is the first dated work of Sienese painting (1215); a frontal by Guido da Siena with the «Transfiguration», «Christ entering Jerusalem» and «the Resurrection of Lazarus», rare painting on canvas of the medieval period; painted Cross of the end of the 12th century and another Cross painted on a board at the beginning of the 13th century.

HALL II: frontal with Saint Peter on the Throne and at its sides six holy stories, attributed to Guido da Siena or his School: panels with stories of Christ, by Guido da Siena, maybe belonging to the «Majesty» preserved in the Public Palace; Virgin Mary with Child and Saints, an early painting by Guido da Siena; a frontal with the Baptist on the Throne, having at its sides stories of his life, painted at the end of the 13th century by a Sienese Byzantine master.

HALL III: polyptych with Virgin Mary with Child and Saint Agnese, Saint John the Evangelist, Saint John the Baptist and Saint Magdalene, painted by Duccio di Buoninsegna and his assistants; the Virgin of Mercy by Niccolò di Segna; Virgin Mary with Child painted by Duccio di Buoninsegna; other important works by Duccio's School, Ugolino di Nerio and Niccolò di Segna.

HALL IV: Virgin of the Franciscan friars, famous painting on board (about 1300) by Duccio di Buoninsegna, painted with refined illuminated technique; important works by Ugolino di Nerio, Master of Città di Castello and Segna di Bonaventura.

HALL V and VI: Virgin Mary with Child, an admirable painting on board attributed to Duccio di Buoninsegna and, maybe, to Simone Martini; Virgin of Mercy, a great masterpiece on board attributed to Simone Martini; The Blessed Soul Agostino Novello and his miracles, another remarkable masterpiece by Simone Martini; Virgin with Child, Angel and Saints by Lippo Memmi,

1. Via San Pietro with Buonsignori Palace, seat of the National Gallery; 2. Hall n. 17 contains works exclusively by Sano di Pietro.

Luca di Tommè, Bartolo di Fredi, by unknown artists and by the School of Simone Martini.

HALL VII: triptych with Virgin and Child, Saint Mary Magdalene and Saint Dorothy, painted by Ambrogio Lorenzetti in the first half of the 14th century: two small boards, «City on the coast» and «Castle on the shore of a lake» by Ambrogio Lorenzetti, very famous not only for their artistic value but also because they are the first entirely landscape paintings which appeared in Europe; Virgin with Child by the same author; Virgin with Child, Saints, Doctors of the Church and Angels, another harmonious masterpiece by Ambrogio Lorenzetti; «Annunciation», the last known masterpiece by

Ambrogio Lorenzetti, signed and dated 1344, with an interesting perspective view; Virgin with Child between Saint Nicholas of Bari and the Prophet Elijah, Stories of the Carmelites friars, San Taddeo and Saint Bartholomew, Saint Thomas and Saint Jacob, on the central part, predella and side parts, respectively, of the large altar-piece painted between 1328 and 1329 by Pietro Lorenzetti for the Church of the Carmine; Nativity of the Virgin with, at her side, Saint Jacob, Saint Catherine of Alexandria, Bartholomew and Elisabeth of Hungary, a work of the end of the 14th century by Paolo di Giovanni Fei; Assumption of the Virgin by Master of San Pietro Ovile; Virgin Mary with Child among the Saints and the Prophet Daniel, work signed by Giovanni Fei; polyptych (1362) by Giacomo di Mino del Pellicciaio.

HALL VIII: Adoration of the Three Wise Men, masterpiece by Bartolo di Fredi, dated between 1370 and 1380; Scenes of Virgin Mary's life, attributed to the same artist; Crucifixion, by Andrea Vanni.

HALL IX: Saint Michael on the Throne and Saints Anthony Abbot and John the Baptist, a painted board by Angelo Puccinelli from Lucca; Crucifixion by Niccolò di Pietro Gerini; Virgin with Child, Nativity and Crucifixion, triptych of 1336 by Bernardo Daddi; Four Evangelists, attributed to Antonio Veneziano; Virgin with Child and Angels, triptych by Lorenzo Monaco.

HALL X: Saints Cosma and Damian, works on board by a Bolognaise author of the end of the 14th century; in the chapel, at the altar a Virgin with the Child and Saint John by Jacopo Alessandro Calvi, end of the 18th century.

2

National Gallery: 1. Our Lady of the Franciscan Friars, by Duccio di Buoninsegna; 2. Virgin with Child, by Simone Martini.

HALL XI: here there are works by Taddeo di Bartolo: Adoration of the Shepherds, Annunciation and Saints, triptych of 1409; Virgin with Child and Saints, Adoration of the Three Wise Men, Virgin Mary with Child and four Saints, polyptych painted by Martino di Bartolomeo; Virgin Mary with Child and Saints, painting by Andrea di Bartolo.

HALL XII: this hall is entirely dedicated to works by Giovanni di Paolo. Inside one finds a small «Majesty»; the Staggia altar-piece; Saint Andrew Apostle; a polyptych signed and dated 1440, the Crucifixion; Saint Mary Magdalene, Saint Galgano, Saint Bernardino, Saint Romualdo, sides of a polyptych and the predella of the polyptych.

HALL XIII: Final Judgement with Paradise and Hell, one of the best works by Giovanni di Paolo; The Last Supper by Sassetta; Saint Anthony Abbot beaten by the Devils, by the same artist; Our Lady of Humbleness, about 1445 by Giovanni di Paolo; Patient and Triumphant Christ, a painted board by the same

artist; Presentation of Mary to the Temple and Flight to Egypt, 1436, also by Giovanni di Paolo; triptych, Virgin Mary with Child and Saint Catherine of Alexandria and Saint John the Baptist, by the Master of the Osservanza.

HALL XIV: here one can find three small painted boards, Putifarre's wife and the pure Joseph, Susan bathing, Joseph sold by his brothers, by Francesco di Giorgio Martini, a masterpiece dated 1475; works by Neroccio di Bartolomeo: Virgin with Child and Saints Girolamo and Bernard, a masterpiece of about 1475; Virgin with Child and Saints Michael and Bernard, signed and dated 1476; Virgin Mary with Child, Magdalene, and the Baptist; Virgin Mary with Child and Saints John the Baptist and Andrew in a 15th century frame. Works by Matteo di Giovanni: Virgin with Child and Angels; Virgin Mary with Child; Virgin with Child and Saints Michael and Magdalene; Virgin with Child and Saints John the Evangelist and James; Virgin with Child and Saints John the Evangelist and Francis. Works by Francesco di Giorgio Martini: Annunciation; Nativity with Saint Bernard and Saint Thomas of Aquinus (1475); Virgin Mary with Child and an Angel; Virgin with Child and Saints Jacob and Gerolamo; Joseph and the wife of Putifar, Susan bathing and Joseph sold, panels from a nuptial chest.

National Gallery: 1. «A town on the coast», by Ambrogio Lorenzetti; 2. Birth of the Virgin Mary, triptych on wooden board. On the sides, Saint Jacob and Saint Catherine of Alexandria, Bartholomew and Elisabeth of Hungary. Work by Giovanni Fei.

HALL XV: Adoration of the Shepherds with Saints Galgano and Martin, by Pietro di Domenico, his only signed work; Adoration of the Shepherds with Saints, by Andrea di Niccolò; Triumph of David, front of a chest, painted by Neroccio di Bartolomeo's School.

HALL XVI: here one finds a collection of works by Sano di Pietro: triptych with «The Assumption of the Holy Virgin», painted on board; the polyptych of the Gesuati, signed and dated 1444; Virgin Mary with Child and eight Angels; Saint Girolamo in the desert. In the same hall, works by Master of the Osservanza: Pietà with the arrest and martyrdom of Saint Bartholomew, predella of a triptych (about 1450); Crucifixion, Saint Ambrogio humiliates Teodosio and Saint Girolamo in the desert, predella of the altar-piece in the Basilica dell'Osservanza.

HALL XVII: in this hall one finds works by Sano di Pietro. Among these can be mentioned: Coronation of the Virgin between four Saints, triptych of the middle of the 15th century; triptych of about 1465 with Virgin Mary with Child, Saint Girolamo, the Blessed Soul Giovanni Colombini, the Saints Cosma and Damian and, in the cusp, Saint Peter and the Annunciation, the Holy Virgin recommending Siena to Pope Callisto the Third.

HALL XVIII: Virgin Mary with

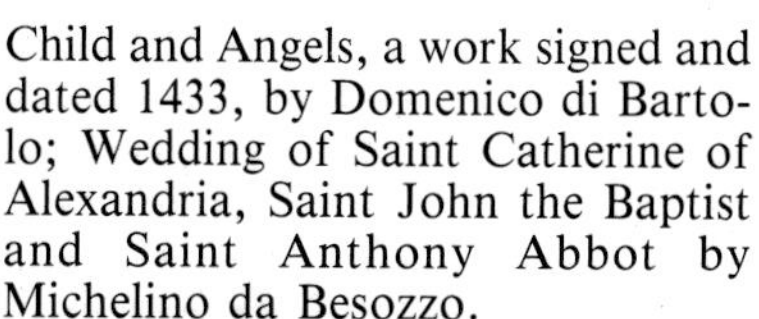

National Gallery: 1. Work by Lorenzo di Pietro, called «il Vecchietta». Detail of two large painted doors of an opening on the wall which contained relics in the large sacristy of the Hospital of Santa Maria della Scala in Siena.

Child and Angels, a work signed and dated 1433, by Domenico di Bartolo; Wedding of Saint Catherine of Alexandria, Saint John the Baptist and Saint Anthony Abbot by Michelino da Besozzo.

HALL XIX: Coronation of the Virgin, a beautiful work by Francesco di Giorgio Martini; Ascension by Benvenuto da Giovanni, 1491; Saint Bernard, below him one of the saint's sermons by Vecchietta; a large painted board, representing the Virgin with Child and Saints Peter, Paul, Lorenzo and Francis, painted by Vecchietta for his own sepulchral chapel; Christ undressed at the Calvary by Francesco di Giorgio Martini.

On the third floor one finds several paintings coming mainly from the Spannocchi collection. There are works of important German and Dutch masters like Albrecht Dürer and Christoph Amberger and Italian masters such as Lotto, Moroni, Padovanino.

On the first floor, which is being re-organised, one can still admire works from the Sienese 16th century School and more recent works. Most of the works found here are by Antonio Bazzi called Sodoma and Domenico di Pace called Beccafumi.

HALL XX: Virgin with Child and Saints Catherine of Alexandria, Augustin, Sebastian and Monica, a work signed and dated 1500, by Andrea di Niccolò; Annunciation by Girolamo da Cremona; Virgin with Child and two Saints by Pacchiarotti; a fresco dated around 1510, «Noli me tangere», by Benvenuto di Giovanni.

HALL XXI: at the present moment this hall is in preparation.

HALL XXII: polyptych, Virgin with Child and four Saints, with a four partitioned predella by Bicci di Lorenzo (1430); Virgin Mary with Child and Angels, a painted board by Neri di Bicci, dated 1482; Assumption of the Holy Virgin, a work probably by the so-called Master Esiguo.

HALL XXIII: Visitation of the Virgin, a painted board by Pietro degli Orioli; Holy Family with Saint John, a «tondo» of exquisite workmanship by Pinturicchio; Ransom of the prisoners and Aeneas fleeing from Troy, detached frescoes, coming from the palace of Pandolfo Petrucci il Magnifico by Gerolamo Genga; Virgin Mary on the throne with Child and Saints, a signed paint-

National Gallery: 1. The small «Majesty» by Ambrogio Lorenzetti; 2. Virgin with Child and Saints Girolamo and Bernard, by Neroccio di Bartolomeo.

ing dated 1512 by Bernardino Fungai; a predella, divided into seven sections with stories of the Bible and Saints, by Pietro degli Orioli.

HALL XXIV: Martyrdom of Saint Martina by Pietro da Cortona; Virgin Mary with Child and Angels, fresco by Rutilio Manetti; Saint George between Faith and Charity, fresco by Ventura Salimbeni.

HALL XXV: Martyrdom of Saint Ansano and Miracle of Saint Eligio, paintings by Rutilio Manetti; the Game of Morra, by Jean du Champ; Betsabea bathing by Lorenzo Lippi.

HALL XXVI: *loggia* (on rearrangement). There are sculptures and bas-reliefs by Sienese artists among which Geno di Fazio and Giovanni d'Agostino.

National Gallery: 1. Holy Family with Saint John, by Pinturicchio; 2. Deposition from the Cross, masterpiece by Giovanni Antonio Bassi, called «Sodoma».

HALL XXVII, XXVIII, XXIX, XXX (on rearrangement): Resurrection, by Giorgio Vasari; the famous portrait of Elizabeth the First, by Cornelio Van Ketel; Charity, Hope and Strength, by Brescianino; Annunciation of the Virgin Mary, by Girolamo del Pacchia; Nativity with Saint John, a famous work by Sodoma (1509); Virgin Mary with Child, by Beccafumi; triptych of the Trinity, an early work by Beccafumi; Saint Catherine of Siena, by Brescianino.

HALL XXXI: a Pietà, by Girolamo di Benvenuto; Judith, a painting by Sodoma; Christ at the Column, a fresco by the same artist; Stigmata of Saint Catherine and Stories of the Saint, an early masterpiece by Beccafumi (1514-1515).

HALL XXXII: four small painted boards by Sodoma, Virgin with Child, The Brothers of the Company of Fontegiusta, again Virgin with Child and Pietà; Deposition of the Cross, a magnificent masterpiece by Sodoma.

HALL XXXIII, XXXIV, XXXV, XXXVI: they are used for temporary exhibitions. When there are no such exhibitions, we can admire cartoons painted by Beccafumi for the floor of the Duomo of Siena.

HALL XXXVII: Saint Michael and the Rebel Angels, unfinished masterpiece by Beccafumi (1528); Christ in Limbo and the Prayer in the Garden, frescoes by Sodoma, coming from the Church of Santa Croce; Christ in Limbo, board by Beccafumi painted between 1530 and 1535; in the centre of the hall there is a wooden group with 18th century gilding, attributed to Jacopo della Quercia, representing the Annunciation.

PIA'S HOUSE

Continuing along San Pietro Street, beyond the Buonsignori Palace, one finds, on the right, the so-called House of Pia dei Tolomei, the old Pannocchieschi Palace. It is an elegant Gothic style Palace, restored in the second half of the 19th century, with a simple façade adorned with two orders of mullioned windows with stone columns and varied capitals. The dedication to Pia dei Tolomei is connected with the sad story, mentioned by Dante in the Divine Comedy, of Pia, widow of Baldo Tolomei, later bride of Nello Pannocchieschi, suspected of adultery and incarcerated, because of this, in Castel di Pietro in Maremma until her death.

National Gallery: 1. The Blessed Agostino Novello and four of his miracles, by Simone Martini (temporarily in deposit); 2. The Blessed Agostino Novello, detail; 3. Annunciation, by Francesco Di Giorgio Martini.

CHURCH OF SAN PIETRO ALLE SCALE

On arrival at the small square and not far from it one finds, at the top of a long stairway, the Church of San Pietro alle Scale or San Pietro in Castelvecchio. The building of 13th century origin was completely rebuilt in the 18th century and appears with

a façade, opened by a gable door, with brickwork decorations and, in the inside, a single nave. Inside the building there are: at the first altar on the right an Assumption by Rustichino; on the main altar, a Flight into Egypt, a beautiful work by Rutilio Manetti (1621); in the close rectory, a Virgin Mary and Santa Lucia with the Archangel Gabriel by Sano di Pietro, Four Saints by Ambrogio Lorenzetti, a Christ Blessing by Giovanni di Paolo and a Virgin Mary by the Lorenzetti's School.

STALLOREGGI STREET

Returning to Postierla Square, one can continue the tour of the City along Stalloreggi Street. It is particularly interesting for its old houses which are elegant architectural examples of decorations and windows. At the corner of Castelvecchio Street there is a remarkable tabernacle with a Pietà by Sodoma frescoed on it: the legend says that, in that spot, in 1438, a crow had fallen dead having inside the germ of pestilence which afterwards upset the town.

The popular title of the fresco derives from this event: the Virgin of the Crow. At number 89/91 of the street there is the house in which Duccio di Buoninsegna painted, between 1308 and 1311, the renowned Majesty. At the end of the street we reach the *Arch of the two Doors* which was a part of the old circle of walls surrounding the town in the 11th century. The arch is decorated with two

1. Via San Pietro; 2. Church of Saint Peter alle Scale; 3. Church of Saint Nicholas al Carmine.

bernacles: the one above on the ght has a Virgin Mary and Saints y Baldassarre Peruzzi, the one outde on the left, a Virgin with Child robably by Memmo di Filippuccio.

HURCH OF SAN ICCOLÒ AL CARMINE

Going out of the Arch, on the left e follow the Pian dei Mantellini. In ont of the *Pollini Palace*, the form- Celsi Palace, planned by Baldasrre Peruzzi and characterized by a rickwork façade lying on a slope ooting and two orders of windows nd a richly decorated cornice, one aches the side of the Church of San iccolò al Carmine. The complex hich comprises the bell tower with our orders and the cloister full of escoes, dates back to the 14th cenry and was altered in the 16th cenry probably according to a plan by aldassarre Peruzzi. The façade is artially covered by the entrance of e old convent in which there is the oister. The inside, of 14th century ppearance, has a single nave covered ith painted trusses and illuminated y windows with ogival arches. Beinning from the right there are inde: an Adoration of the Shepherds, y Duccio di Buoninsegna complet- d by Arcangelo Salimbeni; at the rst altar, an Assumption of Holy Mary, part of a fresco by Gualtiero di Giovanni; at the second, a Saint Michael by Beccafumi; remains of frescoes, an Annunciata, attributed to Ambrogio Lorenzetti and a Virgin with Child, also of the beginning of the 14th century; in the Chapel of the Sacrament on the altar by Marrina, a Nativity of Holy Mary by Sodoma; a painting of the so-called Virgin of the Capes, belonging to the Sienese School with clear Byzantine derivations of the first half of the 13th century, surrounded with Saints by Francesco Vanni. On the main altar of the presbytery there is a marble ciborium of the 16th century. In the apse there is a worshipped small painting of Byzantine style representing the Virgin of the Carmine and two inlaid 16th century doors. Beyond the sacristy, built in 1512 by Vannoccio Biringucci with a plan of Francesco di Giorgio Martini, along the left wall of the nave, one finds: a Martyrdom of Saint Bartholomew by Alessandro Casolani and, on the second altar, an Ascension of Jesus by Girolamo del Pacchia.

CHURCH OF SAINTS PETER AND PAUL

Walking along Pian dei Mantellini and turning towards Diana Street one arrives at the San Marco Street

exit and here one finds the beautiful 18th century façade of the *Oratory of the Virgin of the Rosary*. A little beyond it one can see the old *monastery of Santa Marta* with a 16th century church. Turning into S. Marco Street at No 37, beyond an iron railing, there is the Church of Saints Peter and Paul. The building is a 17th century work by Flaminio del Turco. The façade, preceded by a portico, is made of brickwork, the plan of the inside is in the shape of a Greek cross. At the altars, among rich stucco decorations, one finds: on the right, the so-called Virgin of the Rosary of the 13th century; on the left, a Conversion of Saint Paul by Astolfo Petrazzi and on the main altar, a Coronation of the Virgin Mary by Andrea del Brescianino.

CHAPEL OF THE PRISON OF SAINT ANSANO

Returning to Pian dei Mantellini and taking San Quirico Street, on the right of Pollini Palace, one goes up to a small square in which there is the brickwork façade of the Chapel of the Prison of Saint Ansano. It was built in the 9th century and altered in the 15th century: scholars think it was the first Baptistry in town. In the same small square there is the *tower of Rocchetta*, made of stone and probably of Roman origin. It is identified, as the tradition would have it, with the prison of Saint Ansano.

CHURCH OF SAINT AUGUSTINE

Walking along San Quirico Street one can visit the *Church of the Saints Quirico and Giuditta*. It has a beautiful 13th century portal and inside there are 17th century paintings. Coming back along the street and turning to Tommaso Pendola Street one arrives at San Pietro Street. From here, after the *arch of Saint Augustine* or gate of the arch, old town boundary, one reaches the Lawn of Saint Augustine. It is here that the homonymous church is built.

The Temple was built in 1258 and underwent a first change at the end of the 15th century and a second in 1755. This latter transformed both the inside and the outside and was executed by the architect Luigi Vanvitelli.

The façade is very simple, partly covered by a portico which connects it to the edifice of the ex-convent nearby. The inside is very bright, with a single nave and Latin cross plan. The most interesting works preserved here are: on the right at the first altar, a «Holy Communion of San Girolamo» by Astolfo Petrazzi (1631); at the second altar, a «Crucifix and Saints» by Perugino (1506); at the fourth altar a «Jesus falls under the Cross» by Ventura Salimbeni (1612). Further on one enters the *Piccolomini Chapel* where the most valuable works are kept: at the entrance, a statue of Pius the Second,

a sculpture by Giovanni Duprè (1858); at the marble altar full of decorations there is a masterpiece by Sodoma, «the Epiphany» (1518); on the right there was an altar-piece, now temporarily moved to the Museum of the Opera, representing the «Blessed Soul Agostino Novello» painted splendidly by Simone Martini in about 1330; on the left, a «Slaughter of the Innocents», a work by Matteo di Giovanni signed and dated 1428; in front of the altar, in the lunette, there is a «Virgin Mary on the Throne», a fresco, in poor condition, by Ambrogio Lorenzetti; below, there is a wooden statue, «Virgin with Child» of the 15th century, probably made by Mattia di Nanni di Stefano, called Bernacchino. On the left wall of the nave there is, at the first altar, an «Adoration of the Shepherds» by Giovanni Francesco Romanelli; at the second, an «Immaculate Conception» by Carlo Maratta (1671); at the third, «The Baptism of Constantine» by Francesco Vanni (1586); at the fourth altar, «Saint Augustine and the Angel» by Pietro Sorri (1600).

1. Gate S. Marco; 2. Prato and Church of Saint Augustin; 3. Church of Saint Augustin: Virgin on the Throne; fresco by Ambrogio Lorenzetti.

PIER ANDREA MATTIOLI STREET

From the Lawn of Saint Augustine, going out of the town, one can find a small square where there is the Church of *Santa Mustiola alla Rosa*; on the right, in the *ex-monastery of the Camaldolesi* (look at the beautiful cloister) there are two museums: the Zoological and the Geo-mineralogical, both belonging to the Academy of the Physiocrats. The Academy, founded in 1691 by Pirro Maria Gabrieli, inspired by new economic theories, is still active in the University. Pier Andrea Mattioli Street begins from the small square and in this street there are the Institute and the Botanic Garden; at the end there is the *barrel-vaulted Tufi*, built in 1325 by Agnolo di Ventura.

Walking beyond the gate one reach the *Cemetery of Mercy*, full of scul tures and frescoes, which are moder works by Sienese artists.

CHURCH OF SAINT JOSEPH

Again from the Lawn of Saint A gustine, going to the right along Sa t'Agata Street, one arrives at t Church of Saint Joseph, built in 16 by the Corporation of Joiners, wi a beautiful brickwork façade 1643, made by Benedetto Giovanne and from 1786, entrusted to the Co

1. View of the Arch of San Giuseppe. In t background, the Tower of Mangia; 2. Pr to di Sant'Agostino and Church of Sai Joseph; 3. Fountain of the Contrada d l'Onda.

2

3

trada of the Wave. On the left of the church there is the *Arch of Saint Joseph*, the remains of an old gate, framing the tower of Mangia with Duprè Street in the background. Going along this street one reaches the *market square*, at the back of the Public palace. In this square was once held the cattle market. Until 1346 the market was held in the Square of the Campo.

CHURCH OF SAINT GIROLAMO

Leaving the Market Square, following a stairway and turning into a lane one arrives at Salicotto Street. Going right one crosses the district that once was the Jewish ghetto inside which are lanes, steps, arches and balconies. Next, past the *Oratory of San Giacomo*, built in 1531 in which we find a «Martyrdom of San Giacomo» by Rutilio Manetti (1605) and a «Going to the Calvary» by Sodoma, one takes the first turning on the right and through San Girolamo Street one arrives at the Church of San Girolamo. The 14th century Temple has a single nave and inside we find: on the right, between the first two altars, a tombstone of Bishop Bettini, by Giacomo Cozzarelli (1507); in the left chapel, a «Coronation of the Virgin Mary» by Sano di Pietro (1465); at the third altar on the left, a painting by Marrina of «The Virgin Mary and Saints» by Giuliano da Firenze (1487). In the nearby convent the cloister offers a fresco of the «Assumption» by Bernardino Fungai (1487), having near it figures of «Saints» by Giuliano da Firenze and other frescoes of the end of the 15th century.

CHURCH OF SANTA MARIA DEI SERVI

Through Servi Street, coming from San Girolamo Street, one arrives at Alessandro Manzoni Square where, at the end of a long set of steps, the Church of Santa Maria dei Servi can be seen. It was built during the 13th century and enlarged in the following two centuries. It has an extremely simple brickwork façade, with a single portal and two rose-windows. Beside the façade there is the Romanesque bell tower, restored in this century, with four lines of windows without mullions at the bottom but adding a mullion storey by storey until at the top they become four mullioned windows. The inside of the church has a Latin cross plan with three aisles and marble columns. The project of the aisles, Renaissance style, is attributed to Baldassarre Peruzzi and to Porrina, the actual building to Ventura Turapilli.

2

The transept and the apse are of Gothic style. Inside the most remarkable works are: in the left aisle, close to the first column, a holy water stoup partially dating back to the 13th century; on the outside of the first chapel there are remains of 14th century frescoes; at the second altar, a masterpiece by Coppo di Marcovaldo, signed and dated 1261 and representing a «Virgin with Child and Angels», called the «Virgin of the Bordone», of Byzantine-like style; at the third altar, a «Nativity of the Virgin» by Rutilio Manetti; at the fifth altar a «Slaughter of the Innocents» (1491) and a «Virgin and Saints», by Matteo di Giovanni. Next to the sacristy door a «Virgin with Child» by Segna di Bonaventura. In

the second chapel, on the right of the presbytery, one finds two splendid works: a «Slaughter of the Innocents» by Pietro Lorenzetti and on the altar, the «Virgin of the People» by Lippo Memmi. On the main altar, an altar-piece of the 16th century by Bernardino Fungai representing the «Coronation of Holy Mary». In the second chapel on the left of the presbytery: «Herod's banquet» and «The Trance of Saint John the Evangelist», both works by Pietro Lorenzetti. In the inside of the chapel, placed at the bottom of the left transept, there is «The Virgin of Mercy» by Giovanni di Paolo (1436). Along the left aisle one finds: at the first altar, an «Annunciation» by Francesco Vanni; at the second, between a «Virgin Mary» and a «Saint Joseph», both works by Bernardino Fungai, one finds the «Virgin of Belvedere» by Giacomo di Mino del Pellicciaio (1363).

ORATORY OF THE HOLY TRINITY

In Valdimontone Street, along the left side of the Church of Santa Maria dei Servi, between its transept and apse, there is the oratory of the Holy Trinity. It was built in 1298 and altered at the end of the 16th century. The interior is full of decorations and stuccoes of the 16th and 17th centu-

4

1. Market Square; 2. Church of Santa Maria dei Servi; 3. Church of Santa Maria dei Servi: interior; 4. Virgin with Child and Angels, by Coppo di Marcovaldo.

ries by Prospero Bresciani and Cristoforo Rustici, and rich in frescoes by Raffaele Vanni and Giuseppe Nasini on the side walls, and Ventura Salimbeni in the vault and lunettes. A bronze crucifix (1576) is placed on the altar and, in the right chapel, there is a «Virgin Mary with Child» by Sano di Pietro. Inside a tabernacle in the sacristy there is a «Virgin with Child» and the «Saints Michael and John the Baptist» by Neroccio di Bartolomeo.

ROMA STREET

Through a staircase, Valdimontone Street gives onto Roma Street next to the *Church of the Santuccio* belonging to the complex of the ex-monastery of Santa Maria degli Angeli, built in 1362, but the façade is of 1557. Behind the church there is the building of the Museum of the Company of the Executants of Pious Dispositions. In this museum we find works by Ugolino di Nerio, Sodoma, Girolamo di Benvenuto, Lippo Memmi, Niccolò di Ser Sozzo Tegliacci and other artists.

Walking along Roma Street towards the outskirts of the town one arrives at the *Roman gate*; embattled and with a defensive rampart, it is the mightiest gate in Siena. It was erected in 1327, probably based on a project by Agnolo di Ventura. Some

frescoes by Taddeo di Bartolo, San di Pietro and Sassetta adorned th tower. Now there are visible trace only of the Sassetta fresco under th arch, the «Glory of the Angel Musicians», the sole example of a fresc by this artist. Beyond the gate, a few minutes walk away, it is possible t reach the *Church of Santa Mari degli Angeli*, a 15th century construction.

Coming back the same way an walking again along Roma Stree towards the town centre, at the bottom of a small square on the right one finds the *Church of the Refugio* It was erected in 1598 and has a marble façade with three orders: insid there are works by Domenico di Bartolo, Francesco Vanni, Ventura Salimbeni and Rutilio Manetti. Agai along Roma Street at No 47 there i the *building of San Galgano*, built i the second half of the 15th century with a smooth ashlar façade and tw lines of mullioned windows.

CHURCH OF SANTO SPIRITO

Going on along Pantaneto Stree and turning right to Pispini Stree one arrives at the Renaissanc Church of Santo Spirito. It was constructed in 1498 and is composed o a simple brickwork cabin façade, an a stone portal maybe by Baldassarr Peruzzi (1519). The dome, attributed to Giacomo Cozzarelli, dates bac to 1508. In the small square befor the church there is the Pispini Fountain, built in 1534. Inside one find a single nave and a deep presbitery The dome is placed at the crossing o the church wings.

Along the wall on the right ther is a painted terracotta crib by Ambrogio della Robbia (1504): following on, in the first chapel, called «th Spanish Chapel», there are frescoe and canvasses by Sodoma; the fresco represents Saint Sebastian, Sain Anthony Abbot and Saint James o Compostela riding over the corpse of the beaten Saracens; the canvas Saint Nicholas of Tolentino an Saint Michael, the Archangel. In th second chapel there is a woode statue, «San Vincenzo Ferreri» b

Giacomo Cozzarelli; in the third, a «Coronation of Holy Mary» by Domenico Beccafumi; in the fourth chapel, on the altar, «San Giacinto in Gloria» by Francesco Vanni, and, on the walls, «Stories of the Saints» by Ventura Salimbeni. The apse is adorned with: «Four Saints», on the pillars at the sides of the main altar, by Rutilio Manetti (1608); in the basin, «The Whit Sunday» fresco by Giuseppe Nasini. On the left side: in the third chapel, a wooden crucifix by Sano di Pietro and two wooden statues «San Girolamo» and the «Virgin Mary» by Giacomo Cozzarelli; in the second is another wooden statue, by Cozzarelli, representing Saint Catherine of Siena and, finally, in the first chapel the «Virgin Mary received into Heaven» and «Saint Francis and Saint Catherine of Siena», a 16th century work, attributed to Andrea Balducci. At the end of Pispini Street, walking along the walls and passing by the small *Church of San Gaetano* (second half of the 17th century) one reaches the Pispini Gate, once called the Gate of San Viene, erected in 1326, perhaps based on a project of Minuccio di Rinaldo, decorated with the remains of a fresco representing «the Nativity» by Sodoma (1531).

CHURCH OF SAINT MARTIN

Following Pantaneto Street one passes in front of the *Church of Saint George* on the right. It dates back to the 13th century and was erected to the memory of the Battle of Montaperti and was rebuilt in 1741 with a Baroque travertine façade. The original bell tower is tower-shaped in Romanesque style.

Turning into Magalotti Lane one comes to Porrione Street. At No 49 there is the building of the *Archbrotherhood of Mercy*, the old Company of Saint Anthony, the Abbot, founded halfway through the 13th century, while further on one comes to the Church of Saint Martin. It was erected in 1537 based on a project by Giovanni Battista Pelori, while the stone façade, a mannerist piece of art, was built by Giovanni Fontana in 1613. The plan is of a Latin cross and there is a single nave with a great dome in the middle, frescoed by Annibale Mazzuoli, and a deep presbytery. Along the right nave, one finds: at the second altar, a «Circumcision» by Guido Reni; at the third, held in a rich marble frame of the Marrina School (1522), a «Martyrdom of Saint Bartholomew» by Guercino. In front of this work, there are five wooden gold-plated statues: a «Virgin Mary with Child» by Jacopo della Quercia and the «Saints Peter, Bartholomew, John and Anthony, the Abbot», by the Marrina School, all made between 1419 and 1425. In the right hand part of the transept one finds a statue representing San Tommaso di Villanova by Giovanni Antonio Mazzuoli; on the left hand side there is, on the altar, a «Conception» by Giuseppe Mazzuoli. On the main altar one finds other works by Giuseppe Mazzuoli, statues of angels and saints.

The apse staired-glass window, representing Saint Martin, is by Pastorino dei Pastorini. In the left wall of the nave there are: at the third altar, built by Marrina, a «Nativity» by Beccafumi; at the second, a group of 15th century wooden statues with a crucifix between the Virgin Mary and Saint John, the Evangelist: at the first altar a Saint Ivonne by Raffaele Vanni. The painting next to the entrance represents the Holy Virgin protecting Siena, painted by Lorenzo Cini for the Battle of Camollia (1526).

Church of Refugio.

TOUR OF THE TOWN NO. FOUR

4 *Piccolomini Palace • University • Church S. Maria di Provenzano • Church S. Pietro Ovile • Basilica of S. Francesco • Oratory S. Bernardino • Ovile Gate • New Fountain • Church S. Donato • Salimbeni Square • Tolomei Square • Independence Square • Branda Fountain • Sanctuary S. Caterina • Basilica of S. Domenico • Municipal Library of the Intronati • National Archeological Museum • Church S. Pellegrino alla Sapienza • Camollia Gate • Giusta Fountain • Church S. Pietro alla Magione • S. Barbara*

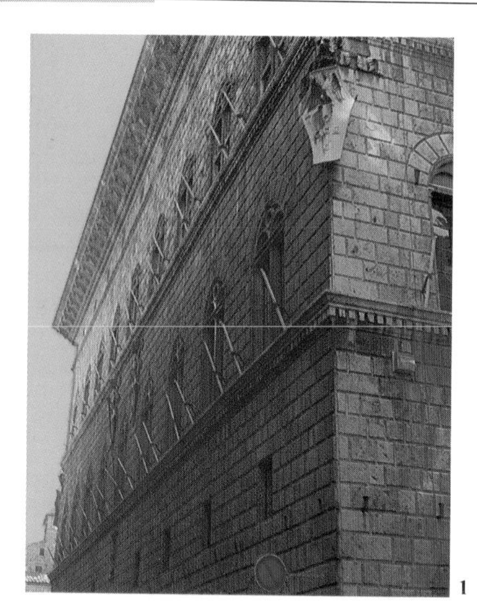

1

PICCOLOMINI PALACE

Along Banchi di Sotto Street, at the corner with Rinaldini Street, which leads to the Square of the Campo, one finds the imposing sight of the Piccolomini Palace. Its style, evidently connected with the Florentine Renaissance, calls to mind the Rucellai Palace in Florence by Leon Battista Alberti and of the Piccolomini Palace by Bernardo Rossellino. The plan of this Palace is attributed to Rossellino too but the works were started in 1469 by Pietro Paolo Porrina. It is a two-floor construction, separated with a marking architrave over-hung by an admirable cornice. The stone façade is treated with smooth ashlar and adorned with two elegant orders of mullioned windows. On the ground floor they are decorated with wrought-iron bangles and coats of arms with the half-moon of the Piccolomini above. The *Archives of State*, lodged in the building, preserve an important collection of historical documents formed in 1775 and arranged here in 1885. The collection comprises over 60,000 parchments, from A.D. 736 on, resolutions and statutes of the Republic, and letters and acts of judicial and financial administration. Three halls contain the most interesting part of them: documents referring to personages and events recalled by Dante in the Divine Comedy, the Last Will of Giovanni Boccaccio, Imperial diplomas from 818, papal bulls from 992, autographic documents of renowned personages and artists, documents referring to famous works of art, historical and commercial documents, and a collection of illuminated statutes and illuminated manuscripts from the 12th to the 17th centuries. The most important collection among all the others is the collection of the small *paintings of Biccherna*. It is a series of small painted boards used as covers for the books published by the Magistrates

2

of Biccherna and of the Gabella (tax). They were published every six months and contained the acts of the Republic Financial Administration at the end of each cycle of management. The coat of arms of the magistrates were painted on these books together with a symbolic or holy scene recalling the most outstanding event of that period. The paintings belong to a period between 1258 and 1659 and were painted by the best artists of that age. Among them were Ambrogio and Pietro Lorenzetti, Taddeo di Bartolo, Giovanni di Paolo, Vecchietta, Sano di Pietro, Francesco di Giorgio Martini, Guidoccio Cozzarelli, Domenico Beccafumi and Neroccio di Bartolomeo Landi. Besides these there are other small paintings of other institutions and Town boards preserved.

1. Piccolomini Palace, seat of the State Archives; 2. State Archives: «The Woman with the gold-embroidered mantle» by Taddeo di Bartolo; 3. State Archives: the Virgin protects Siena during earthquakes (1467), by Francesco di Giorgio Martini.

UNIVERSITY

In front of the Piccolomini Palace there is the ex-convent San Vigilio (16th century) that, from 1815, has been the seat of the University. The Sienese Studio, one of the oldest in Italy, already existed at the beginning of the 13th century, by a decision of the Siena Council. It became renowned when, in 1321, the teachers and the pupils of the University of Bologna moved there. Afterwards, in 1357, it obtained by grant of the Emperor Charles the Fourth the privile-

1

2

ges of the Studio Generale. Its fame was great until it diminished during the Grand Duchy of Leopoldo the First; it ceased activities in 1814. The University started to operate again in 1884 under the current arrangement, initiated by institutions and private citizens.

THE POPE'S LOGGIAS

Again in Banchi di Sotto Street, going away from the Square of the Campo, one finds, on the right, next to the Church of San Martino, the Pope's Loggias. They were erected in 1462 according to a design of Antonio Federighi following the will of the Pope Pius the Second, Enea Silvio Piccolomini, who did much to embellish the town with works of art and Palaces. The Loggias were used as a meeting place of the outstanding Sienese families for important occasions and events. The building, composed of three ample stone arcades over slim Corinthian columns with a high architrave strip, represents a good example of Renaissance architecture.

Passing on the old *Fonte di Pantaneto*, turning left to Follonica Street, one arrives at the small square in which is placed the 13th century *Church*, rebuilt in the 16th century, of *San Giovanni Battista della Scala* or San Giovannino. From here one can walk along Sallustio Bandini Street, a characteristic street of the Sienese Middle Ages, and then San Vigilio Street and the lane of Castellare arriving at the *Court of Castellare degli Ugurgieri*, a perfectly preserved medieval environment.

CHURCH OF SANTA MARIA DI PROVENZANO

Again one begins from Sallustio Bandini Street walking on and turning right to Lucherini Street getting to the small square of the Church of Santa Maria di Provenzano. It was built in 1594 by Flaminio del Turco based on a project by the Carthusian, Damiano Schifardini. The white stone façade is subdivided into two parts by an overhanging moulding. The dome stands on a high octagonal based tambour. In the inside one can see a single nave and a Baroque architecture and the following works: from the right, at the first altar, San Cerbone by Rutilio Manetti (1630); on the pillars of the dome three flags taken from the Turks during the 17th and 18th centuries and one from the Chinese Boxers in 1901: in the right transept, a «Vision of Saint Catherine», by Francesco Rustici; in the tabernacle over the main altar, the

1. Courtyard and portico of the University.
2. Church of Santa Maria di Provenzano.
3. Basilica of Saint Francis.

3

Virgin Mary of Provenzano, a worshipped relief image of the 15th century. Once it was a part of a Pietà kept in the house of Provenzano Salvani; in the left transept a crucifix between the Saints Mary Magdalene and John the Evangelist, sculptures of the 17th century: in the sacristy a «Holy Virgin», a fresco by the Sienese School of the 14th century, a «Holy Family» by Francesco Vanni, a Dedication of the Church, a 14th century work, a Pietà by Cristofano Casolani and beautiful inlaid cupboards.

CHURCH OF SAN PIETRO OVILE

Following the left side of the Church of Santa Maria di Provenzano and turning right to Giglio Street, one arrives at the old Church of San Pietro Ovile, transformed in the 18th century, in which valuable pieces of art are preserved: at the right altar, a 15th century Matteo di Giovanni's copy of Simone Martini's «Annunciation» which is kept in the Florence Uffizi: in the apse, a crucifix by Giovanni di Paolo: at the altar on the left of the main one of the two wooden statues, Virgin Mary and Saint John the Evangelist by Domenico di Niccolò dei Cori (1415); at the left altar, a «Virgin Mary with Child», a beautiful work by the so-called Master of San Pietro Ovile.

BASILICA OF SAINT FRANCIS

Passing along San Pietro Ovile Street and then Rossi Street, on the right, in which one finds a compact line of 13th and 14th centuries buildings, one reaches the *Arch of Saint Francis* with marble 14th century statues above and enters the large square of the Basilica of Saint Francis.

The church construction started in 1326, in the same place in which there was a small church, according to the fundamental rules of the Gothic architecture. The central body of the complex was ended in 1475, probably according to the plan of Francesco di Giorgio Martini. The building suffered a fire in 1665 and then it was altered with Baroque forms and recovered its original style through the restoration of Giuseppe Partini from 1885 on.

The brickwork façade was built between 1894 and 1913 according to the plan of Vittorio Mariani and Gaetano Ceccarelli, while the bell tower date back to 1765 and is by

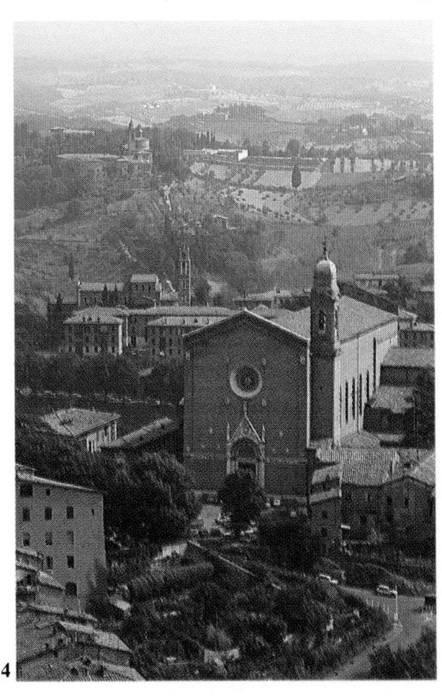

4

1

Paolo Posi. The inside of the Temple is extremely interesting: it is arranged with an Egyptian cross and a single large nave with black and white striped walls. The sheltered part has trusses. Here the natural lighting is provided by mullioned windows and, in the apse, by a large window with four mullions and a stained-glass window. One finds very interesting works of art inside the church. At the entrance, on the right, tomb fragments of the 14th century can be seen. In the first lunette on the right wall there are 15th century frescoes, «The Visitation» and «Saints», and, in the following niche, other images of Saints, frescoes by the 14th century Sienese School. After the side entrance one can see the Tomb of Tolomei, relocated here from another place. Legend has it that the tomb slab in the floor belongs to Pia dei Tolomei. In the sacristy there is a basin of the 16th century decorated with angels by Sodoma. At the head of the right arm of the transept there is a statue of Saint Francis attributed to Francesco di Valdambrino. In the presbytery one finds: in the second chapel, on the right, the tomb of Cristoforo Felici, made by Urbano da Cortona in 1462; in the first chapel, a «Virgin Mary with Child» by Andrea Vanni; on the left wall, two portraits dedicated to the parents of Pius the Second, Vittoria Forteguerri and Silvio Piccolomini, of the 15th century, the only pieces of art which remain on their tombs.

Left transept: in the first chapel, a beautiful detached fresco of a «Crucifixion» by Pietro Lorenzetti (first half of the 15th century): in the third, two detached frescoes, San Ludovico D'Angiò in front of Boniface the Eighth and a Martyrdom of six Francescan friars in Ceuta, beautiful

2

vorks by Ambrogio Lorenzetti (first ıalf of the 14th century, too). In the ıixth chapel of the left wall a Marri-ıa Graphite floor. Through the side loor one descends to a harmonious cloister: at the bottom of it there is ı Renaissance portal, an old connect-ng passage with the ex-convent of Saint Francis. This convent, placed on the right of the Basilica, was built during the 15th century and enlarged n the 16th. The complex stands round a great Renaissance cloister ınd it is today the seat of a faculty of the University.

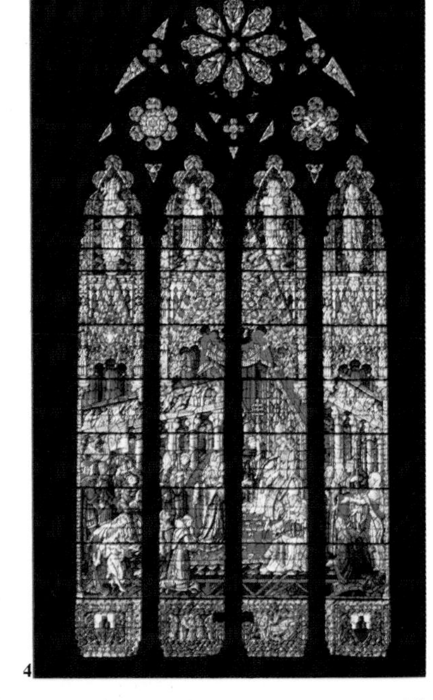

1. Cloister and bell tower of Saint Francis; 2. Interior view; 3. Martyrdom of Six Fran-ciscan Friars, by Ambrogio Lorenzetti; 4. Stained-glass window.

ORATORY OF SAINT BERNARDINO

On the right side of the square there is the Oratory of Saint Bernardino, built in the 15th century in the place in which the Saint used to hold his sermons. The building is composed of two oratories, one upon the other and both full of remarkable works. In the lower one, decorated with 16th century paintings, one finds: next to the altar, a «Virgin with Child and Saints» by Brescianino: in the niches, at the sides, two terracotta statues painted in white, representing Saint Bernardino and Saint Catherine. At the entrance of the upper floor: in the entrance lunette, a wooden polychrome statue, «Virgin with Child», by the School of Jacopo della Quercia: at the altar, a «Virgin Mary» by Sano di Pietro: on the left a gonfalon painted on two sides by Francesco Vanni: on the right, a «Virgin with Child and Angels», a bas-relief by Giovanni d'Agostino.

The upper oratory, with stucco[e]d wood walls and ceiling, decorated b[y] Ventura Turapilli in 1496, ha[s] preserved extremely valuable fresco[es] separated by pillars. They are, begi[nning]

3

ning from the left corner of the wall facing the entrance: «San Ludovico», by Sodoma; «Nativity of Mary», by Girolamo del Pacchia; «Presentation of Mary to the Temple» by Sodoma; «Weddings» by Domenico Beccafumi; «Saint Bernardino» by Girolamo del Pacchia; «the Archangel Gabriel» by the same author; «Virgin Mary in Glory with Saints» by Domenico Beccafumi (1537); the «Blessed Holy Virgin» by Girolamo del Pacchia; «Saint Anthony of Padua» by Sodoma (1518); «Visitation» by the same author; «The Death of Mary» by Domenico Beccafumi (1518); «The Assumption» by Sodoma (1532); «Saint Francis of Assisi» by Sodoma, maybe the most beautiful fresco of the Oratory; «The Coronation of Mary» also by Sodoma.

Oratory of Saint Bernardino: 1. Presentation of Mary to the Temple, by Sodoma; 2. Presentation of Mary to the Temple (detail); 3. Coronation of Mary, by Sodoma.

OVILE GATE-FONTE NUOVA

Coming back into the walls from the Arch of Saint Francis one finds oneself again on Comune Street (along which, on the right, stands the 17th century *Oratory of the Visitation*), one then arrives at Ovile Gate. Over the 14th century gate, built with a rampart, one reaches the Fonte Ovile, an ogival construction dating back to 1262. Coming back to the town along Pian d'Ovile Street is Fonte Nuova. It was erected with three great brickwork ogival arches in the 14th century by Camaino di Crescentino and Sozzo di Rustichino. From here, along Fonte Nuova Street, one arrives at Vallerozzi Street at the *Church of San Rocco*, in which there are paintings of 17th century Sienese artists, and, in the chapel, the «Stories of San Rocco» by Rutilio Manetti and Francesco Rustici.

CHURCH OF SAN DONATO

Walking down Vallerozzi Street and turning left into Abbadia Street one arrives at the Church of San Donato facing the square and the characteristic rear brickwork façade held between two mighty towers of the Salimbeni Palace. It was erected in 1119, as a Vallombrosan Abbey of Saint Michael and passed on to the Carmelites in 1683. They effected several radical transformations. Only the stone and brickwork with a beautiful rose-window and the lower part of the apse were not touched. The only original part remaining in the single nave plan inside is the high tiburium above the arcades and corner walls. These are remarkable works: above on the right a 14th century fresco of the Sienese School: a«Virgin with Child» by Luca Tommè; on the main altar a «Tabernacle and sculptured angels» by Giuseppe Mazzuoli; in the apse, «Saint Michael», a fresco by Luigi Ademollo; in the sacristy, four coffin boards by Sodoma. In the nearby 18th century Oratory of Saints Nails are other coffin boards, attributed to Riccio, and a «Virgin Mary» by Andrea Vanni.

SALIMBENI SQUARE

Coming back to Vallerozzi Street and turning left along Montanini Street, one arrives at the *Oratory of Santa Maria delle Nevi*, a building of 1471 attributed to Francesco di Giorgio Martini. It is characterized by a simple and elegant Renaissance façade with a single portal and simple interiors with small windows: a great masterpiece stands out at the main altar, the «Virgin of the Snows» by Matteo di Giovanni (1477). Along Montanini Street, passing between two medieval towers, one enters Salimbeni Square. On three sides important buildings face the square: in the middle, the monument to Sallustio Bandini, by Tito Sarocchi (end of the 19th century). On the right side there is the *Spannocchi Palace*, built for Ambrogio Spannocchi, treasurer of Pope Pius the Second, begun in 1470, according to a plan by Giuliano da Maiano and later on restored and completed in 1880 by Giuseppe Partini. The Renaissance building has rectangular windows in the façade, and on the ground floor and above there are two orders of mullioned windows. On the top there is a multidegreed cornice. The interior yard, altered by Partini, is adorned with loggias and extremely well-made capitals. On the opposite side there is the *Tantucci Palace*, a Renaissance work by Riccio, which was started work on in 1548. Between the two edifices there is *Salimbeni* Gothic *Palace*, built in the 14th century, enlarged and restored in 1879 by Giuseppe Partini. It has three floors: on the first there is an order of three-

mullioned windows with ogival arches bearing heraldic coats of arms.

It is the seat of Monte dei Paschi di Siena, an old crediting bank, founded in 1624 and incorporating Monte Pio (1472), which operated with the guarantee of the incomes of the «Paschi» of the Sienese Maremma. In the inside one can visit the old warehouse of the Salimbeni Family and see precious documents, seals, management books connected with the economic history of the town and, moreover, several old and new works of art.

TOLOMEI SQUARE

One can continue along Banchi di Sopra Street and pass in front of *Gori Pannilini Palace*, a 1577 project by Giovanni Fontana, of the *Cinughi Palace*, a brickwork Gothic construction with two orders of mullioned windows, of the *Bichi Ruspoli*, having at its sides two incomplete towers of 1520, and then arrive at the spot of Tolomei Square. Here, in front of an old column with a tin she-wolf on the top, stands the *Tolomei Palace*, the oldest Palace in Siena: it already existed in 1205 and was rebuilt, without alteration to the ground floor, in 1267. It is peculiar for the solidity of the architecture, built entirely with stone. It bears, on the two upper floors of the façade, two widely spaced orders of elegant mullioned windows with trilobed lancet arches, marked by string-course cornices.

In front of Tolomei Palace stands the *Church of Saint Christopher*, dating back to the Romanesque age; it was completely altered in 1720. The Council of the Republic held its meetings there before the construction of the Public Palace. Two 19th century statues are placed on the brickwork façade, which is marked by four columns. One can see in the single nave interiors: a wooden crucifix, covered with leather, of the 14th century and the partition of an altarpiece, attributed to Sano di Pietro, representing Saint Christopher and Saint George killing the dragon. Behind the Saint Christopher Romanesque apse, walking towards Moro Street, between the left side of the church and the *Palmieri Nuti Palace* (1540), one arrives at an interesting small brickwork 12th century cloister.

2.

1. Salimbeni Palace and Square; 2. Tolomei Palace and Square.

INDIPENDENZA SQUARE

From Città Street and along Terme Street one enters Independence Square. At No 15 one can see the edifice of the *Academy of the Rozzi*. Founded in 1531 as a Confraternity, it became an Academy in 1691; it was created in opposition to the Aristocratic Academy of the Intronati, operating mainly in the field of theatre. In fact the theatre of the Rozzi can be found very close to the Academy. The theatre was built with a small and elegant hall in 1816 according to a project by Alessandro Doveri and it was restored in 1874. In the same square is the *Loggia of the Indipendenza*, built, in 1887, to a design by Archimede Vestri. At the back of the Loggia there is the medieval *Ballati Palace*, embattled and with a high stone tower.

1

FONTE BRANDA

Along Diacceto Street and on the right is Galluzza Street, a characteristic and picturesque minor medieval street crossed with eight arches, the first with a beautiful two mullioned window. On the left, along the lane of Costaccino, one arrives at Fonte Branda Street in which, a few steps away from the gate bearing the same name, there is the old Fonte Branda. It is rightly considered the most famous of the city fountains and was already known in 1081 and then enlarged in 1198 by Bellamino and rebuilt with its present shape by Giovanni di Stefano in 1246. It is a brickwork construction composed of three ogival arches crowned with a battlement. The front of the Fonte is adorned with four leonine gargoyles and the Siena coat of arms.

The apse wall of the Basilica of San Domenico overlooks the Fonte.

SANCTUARY OF SAINT CATHERINE

To the right of the Fonte Branda and taking the lane of Tiratoio to No 15 is the entrance of the Sanctuary of Saint Catherine. The edifice was once the dwelling place of the saint and was turned into a sanctuary in 1464. It has a Renaissance stone portal and

2

a gracious brickwork small loggia with stone columns.

Caterina Benincasa (1347-1380), daughter of Jacopo, who belonged to the Corporation of the Wool, and of Donna Lapa, was one of the most outstanding personages of her age especially in the passionate fervour which pushed her to renew incisively the Church towards a universal vision.

She is the authoress of a rich collection of letters, a literary document and a mystic testimony, and was a renowned personage. It was she who

rsuaded Pope Gregory the Ninth to
me back to Rome from Avignon
1377. She was canonized by Pius
e Second in 1461 and was
oclaimed Patron Saint of Italy by
us the Twelfth in 1939. After her
nonization her house was turned
to a sanctuary by adding and
anging the structure and by build-
g the Lower Oratory, in which
ere was her father's dyeing cham-
r and the Upper or Kitchen Ora-
ry, the Crucifix Oratory, over the
rden, and the Oratory of the Room
the Saint. The tour takes one to
e upper floor, in the Upper Orato-
, with a lacunar ceiling and gilded
se-windows, a 1594 restoration,
d a maiolica floor of the 17th cenry.
On the altar there is a Bernardino
ngai painting representing Saint
therine Stigmatized. Over the Re-
issance rooms on the walls there
e several remarkable paintings
nong which, starting from the left
le of the altar: «Jesus shows the Saint a cross that she had donated to a poor man» by Sodoma School; «The Holy Communion of the Saint» by Pomarancio; «The Saint exorcises a possessed person» by Pietro Sorri; «The Saint illuminated by the Holy Spirit» by Rutilio Manetti; «Canonization of the Saint» by Francesco Vanni; «The Saints have the vision of Jesus at the column» by Rutilio Manetti; «Gregory The Ninth takes

4

Branda Fountain; 2. Via della Galluzza; Sanctuary of Saint Catherine; 4. Sanctu- of Saint Catherine: courtyard and well.

the Papal seat back in Rome» by Pomarancio. Crossing the small loggia, a work attributed to Baldassarre Peruzzi, one enters the Oratory of the Crucifix. In this hall one finds mainly frescoes by Giuseppe Nasini and also: at the left altar, the «Apotheosis of Saint Catherine» by Rutilio Manetti; at the right altar, «Saint Catherine and Gregory the Ninth» by Sebastiano Conca; at the main altar, a Crucifix on a board by the Pisan School of the beginning of the 13th

Sanctuary of Saint Catherine: 1. Galler leading to the upper Oratory and to the Ora tory of the Crucifix, attributed to Baldas sarre Peruzzi; 2. Upper Oratory; 3. Orato ry of the Crucifix.

century, coming from the Church of Saint Christine of Pisa, in front of which Catherine received the stigmata. Going down to the ground floor and entering the Oratory of the Room of the Saint, there are seven stories of the Saint on the walls, 1896 frescoes by Alessandro Franchi and, at the altar, «The Saint receives the stigmata» by Girolamo di Benvenuto. Next to the Oratory there is the cell in which the Saint lived and objects that belonged to her can still be found there. Going further down one arrives on the right, at the *Church of Saint Catherine in Fonte Branda* or Oratory of the Contrada, the old draper's shop of Jacopo Benincasa. In the only room, covered with a cross-vault, one finds: a wooden polychrome statue of Saint Catherine by Neroccio (15th century) overhung by five angels, by Sodoma, and a painting, «Saint Catherine Stigmatized», by Girolamo del Pacchia; on the right another two frescoes by Girolamo del Pacchia and, on the left, two canvasses by Vincenzo Tamagni and Ventura Salimbeni, representing stories of the Saint. In the next room another 13th century statue of Saint Catherine.

THE BASILICA OF SAN DOMENICO

Going out along Saint Catherine Street, one turns left towards the slope of Saint Anthony and again left towards Sapienza Street. In this way one arrives at San Domenico Square, in which rises the great mass of the Basilica of San Domenico.

The building works were started in 1226 according to the wish of the Dominican friars: the nave and the uncovered trusses roof belong to that period.

The large crypt was built at the beginning of the 14th century. It was called Chiesa di Sotto or Church of the Dead Men. The basilica was completed in 1465 and had to be restored, owing to fire damage, in 1532 by Domenico Cinquini. The church bell tower, built in 1340, stands out on the right of the church. It was reduced in size at the beginning of the 18th century and crowned with battlements at the end of the same century. The architecture is in severe massive Gothic style, completely in brickwork. The Egyptian cross plan inside is as imposing, simple and majestic as the outside.

The visit begins in the Vaults' Chapel, through two ample arcades placed at the bottom right of the nave. Here Saint Catherine wore the Mantellate dress in 1363. Next to the altar one can see a fresco, by Andrea Vanni, a contemporary of the Saint, which is considered the only exact portrait of Saint Catherine. On the bottom wall is a «Canonization of Saint Catherine» by Mattia Preti. Along the right wall of the nave one finds: at the first altar, the «Apparition of the Virgin Mary to the Blessed Soul Andrea Gallerani» by Stefano Volpi; then a 14th century wooden crucifix and a Pietà, polychrome terracotta, of the 16th century; at the second altar, a «Nativity of Mary» by Alessandro Casolani (1584); and, above, a painted board representing Saint Bernardino (15th century).

Then one reaches the Chapel of Saint Catherine, full of works of art: above the entrance-arch, «San

1. Basilica of Saint Dominic; 2. Basilica of Saint Dominic: the nave; 3. Saint Catherine of Siena, by Andrea Vanni.

Girolamo and San Luca», frescoes by Sodoma and, below, the «Blessed Souls Raimondo da Capua and Tommaso Nacci», painted in oils on the wall by Francesco Vanni; on the altar, a marble tabernacle by Giovanni di Stefano (1466) containing the Saint's head; on the right of the altar, the «Ecstasy of Saint Catherine» and, on the left, the «Saint Faints Away», two masterpieces by Sodoma (1526): on the left wall, still by Sodoma, the «Saint Pleads on Behalf of the Salvation of a Tortured Man's Soul»; on the right wall, the «Saint exorcises a Possessed Woman», oil painting by Francesco Vanni (1593). One notices also the grotesque paintings on the pillars and the 16th century marble floor. One continues walking along the nave, near the sacristy door where one finds: «Adoration of the Shepherds», by Francesco di Giorgio Martini; in the lunette, a «Pietà» by Matteo di Giovanni, with a predella by Bernardino Fungai. From the right wall of the nave a staircase leads to the Crypt. It was built at the beginning of the 14th century, as partial foundation of the church, was neglected and recovered only in 1935. It is composed of a single, large room, divided into three naves covered with

3

several cross-vaults, supported by pilasters. A great cross stands on the main altar painted by Sano di Pietro; in the left aisle, in the chapel, a painted board representing the «Holy Father and Four Saints» by Sodoma and others. A painted board representing the «Virgin Mary» is in

the middle of the other figures: it dates back to the second half of the 14th century and was uncertainly attributed to Paolo di Giovanni Fei or to Francesco Vannuccio and, at the bottom, «Crucifixion and Saints» by Ventura Salimbeni; on an altar in the right aisle is a wooden statue of Saint Anthony Abbot attributed to Turino di Sano. Going up again in the right transept one finds: at the third chapel a «Virgin with Child and Saints», a monochrome sketch of the beginning of the 16th century; in the second, the Chapel of the Germans, graves of German people, mostly University students who died in Siena during the 16th and 17th centuries; in the first chapel, «Virgin with Child and Angels» by Matteo di Giovanni. At the main altar a splendid marble ciborium and Two Candelabra-bearing Angels by Benedetto da Maiano, of the end of the 15th century. In the left transept: in the first chapel: a «Virgin with Child», by Sano di Pietro; in the second, masterpieces by Matteo di Giovanni (1479); a «Saint Barbara on the Throne among Angels» and the «Saints Magdalene and Catherine», and, above, an «Epiphany», while, in the same chapel, there is the «Virgin with Child and Four Saints» and, above, a «Pietà» by Benvenuto di Giovanni (1483); in the third chapel, there is a wooden 15th

Basilica of Saint Dominic: 1. Chapel of Saint Catherine, almost entirely frescoed by Sodoma; 2. The Fainting of the Saint; 3. The Saint frees a possessed woman.

century Crucifix. In the left wall of the nave there are: at the fourth altar, a «Virgin with Child, Saint John the Baptist and a Knight on his Knees», a detached fresco and a good work by Pietro Lorenzetti; at the third, «Saint Anthony Abbot exorcises a Possessed Woman» by Rutilio Manetti; at the second, «Mystic Weddings of Saint Catherine of Alexandria» by a disciple of Alessandro Casolani and, finally, at the first altar a «San Giacinto» by Francesco Vanni.

On the right side of the basilica façade there is the 15th century cloister in which some frescoes by Lippo Memmi and Andrea Vanni have been found.

MUNICIPAL LIBRARY OF THE INTRONATI

From San Domenico Square, along Sapienza Street there is, at No 5, the Municipal Library of the Intronati. Created in 1759, the Library is connected with the literary activities of the Academy of the Intronati, founded in about 1525. Over 300,000 volumes are collected here. Among them are to be found important and precious collections of incunabula, manuscripts and curious as well as a 10th century Byzantine Evangelistary, Letters of Saint Paul, 11th century, a 1465 Roman missal, a pontifical and so on.

NATIONAL ARCHAEOLOGICAL MUSEUM

Following the same street one finds the building which houses the National Archaeological Museum. This Museum, founded in 1956, and composed mainly of the Bargagli-Petrucci collection, enriched later with the Bonci-Casuccini and Chigi-Zonzadari collections and other findings, preserves archaeological objects from the Sienese territory. They document the evolution of the civilization in this area, from the prehistoric age to the Roman one. It is subdivided into

three sections: the first hall holds prehistoric findings; then there are the Etruscan and Roman halls holding objects dating from the 7th century B.C. to the 3rd century A.D., from the second to the 10th hall. The last hall houses a collection of old coins, from Etruria, from Piceno, from Umbria, from Lazio and Roman ones.

During the publication of the present guide, the Museum is being moved to new halls inside the Spedale of Santa Maria della Scala.

CHURCH OF SAN PELLEGRINO ALLA SAPIENZA

At the corner of Sapienza Street with Terme Street there is the Church of San Pellegrino alla Sapienza. In the same place, in 1240, there was a chapel dedicated to Saint Mary of Mercy. In 1767 it was altered and took its present shape. The interior, composed of a hall and a nave with Baroque decorations, holds works of the 14th and 15th centuries.

TOWARDS CAMOLLIA GATE

Continuing along the slope of th Incrociata, turning left into Termin Street and then right one arrives a Montanini Street. Along this street heading north-westwards, axis of th «Camollia terziere», one goes pas small palaces founded in the Middl Ages, like *Costantini Palace* (15t century), and one reaches th Romanesque *Church of Saint An drew*, completely altered in the 18t century. Inside the church, at th main altar, one sees a triptych b Giovanni di Paolo (1445), represent ing a «Coronation of the Virgi Mary between Saint Peter and Sain Andrew». Taking Garibaldi Stree one gets to the *Church of the Com*

1. Travertine urn from Perugia, end of 3r - beginning 2nd cent. B.C.. Gift of Bichi Ruspoli-Forteguerri; 2. Small Hellenisti crowned head in clay from the Magna Gre cia. Chigi-Zondadari collection; 3. Front o a Roman sarcophagus with the hunting o a lion, 3rd cent. A.D.. Bargagli-Petrucci co lection. 4. Gate Camollia; 5. Church of Fon tegiusta; nave and main altar.

pany of St. Sebastian. The work was begun at the end of the 15th century and ended in the 17th. Among rich Baroque decorations are frescoes with the stories of Saint Sebastian, by Pietro Sorri, Sebastiano Folli, Cristoforo Casolani, Rutilio Manetti and other artists. On the altar is the wooden Crucifix, which belonged to Saint Bernardino. Other works are: a copy of the «Company of the Gonfalone», painted by Sodoma in 1525 and preserved, from 1786, in Pitti Palace in Florence; and there is a Virgin Mary, in the right chapel, by Francesco Rustici.

One walks along Garibaldi Street again and takes Camollia Street, along which one can find an old Gothic house, a property of the Chigi-Saracini Family, and the *Church of St. Bartholomew*, dating back to the 12th century and then modified.

CHURCH OF FONTEGIUSTA

On the left of Camollia Street one can see the Arch of Fontegiusta crossing which, along the street bearing the same name, one reaches the Church of Fontegiusta. The construction dates back to 1482-1484 and the project was by Francesco Fedeli and Giacomo di Giovanni. The Renaissance façade is made of brickwork and the portal is decorated with marble cornices, made by Urbano da Cortona in 1489: the bas-reliefs placed above, representing the «Virgin Mary among Angels and Garlands», have been attributed to Urbano da Cortona or Neroccio. The interior receives light from the ogival windows and has a square plan. It is divided into aisles by four columns, covered by a cross-vault.

The large-window of the entrance

5

wall dates back to the 15th century and was made according to a design by Guidoccio Cozzarelli. It represents the «Holy Virgin with Child between St. Catherine and St. Bernardino». Other works are: in the arch on the right of the entrance, a «Visitation» by Riccio; at the corner, a 15th century bronze ciborium, attributed to Giovanni delle Bombarde; in the arch of the left aisle, «Jesus, Holy Mary and two Saints», attributed to Francesco Vanni; at the right altar, a «Coronation of Blessed Mary and four Saints», by Bernardino Fungai; following on, a 1510 choir book; on the main altar, a marble tabernacle by Marrina contains a 14th century fresco representing a «Virgin Mary with Child»; in the upper lunette an «Assumption» by Girolamo di Benvenuto (1515); on the left, a bronze Holy-water stoup by Giovanni delle Bombarde (1430); in the arcade, the «Sybil foretells to Augustus the Nativity of the Redeemer», a work of the first half of the 16th century by Baldassarre Peruzzi; a wooden statue of St. Sebastian, 15th century; and, finally, in the last arcade, the «Plague of Siena», by Riccio.

CHURCH OF SAN PIETRO ALLA MAGIONE

One gets back to Camollia Street and finds on the left at the top of a flight of steps the Church of San Pietro alla Magione. Erected in the 14th century by the Order of the Templars and then passed to the order of the Knights of Malta, it was restored completely in 1942. The hewn stone façade has a Gothic portal, while on the right side a brickwork Renaissance chapel leans forward. The single nave inside is extremely interesting, having a truss cover and a presbytery made higher with high and narrow windows. The hewn stone walls are frescoed with fragments of biblical stories, painted monochrome at the end of the 14th century.

1. Church of Fontegiusta: lunette above the main altar, with the Assumption by Girolamo di Benvenuto; 2. La Lizza: park with monument to G. Garibaldi; 3. Northern walls of the Fortress built in 1560 by order of Cosimo I, with stemma of the Medici family.

2

3

The street ends at the *Camollia gate*. It takes the road to Florence, dating back to the 14th century. It was rebuilt in 1604, on a project by Alessandro Casolani.

FORT OF SAINT BARBARA

One walks back again along the Camollia Street to the turning on the right along Gazzani Street. Here one finds on the left the *Church of Santo Stefano alla Lizza*, erected in the 12th century and altered in 1641. Inside one finds: at the right altar, a «Visitation» by Rutilio Manetti; at the main altar a «Virgin Mary with Child and Angels», a polyptych by Andrea Vanni, 15th century, with a predella by Giovanni di Paolo; at the left altar, a wooden St. Bartholomew by Guido del Tonghio.

One goes along the *Lizza*, a Municipal park landscaped at the end of the 18th century, leading to the entrance of the Fort of St. Barbara or Medici's Fortress. It was built according to the will of Cosimo the First in 1560 on a project by Baldassarre Langi. It has a rectangular plan with strong bulwarks at the corners. In 1937 the terraces were converted into a Municipal park, while the rampart houses the Italic Museum of Wine, an exhibition of the Italian vintage wines.

Noble Contrada of the Eagle

The symbol of the contrada is the black imperial eagle, two-headed and crowned, bearing on its breast a sun with the initials U.I., awarded in 1887 by the King of Italy, Umberto, in the year of his presence at the Palio. The colours of the flag are black and sky-blue edged with yellow. The seat is in Casato di Sotto Street and the church is San Giovanni Battista dei Tredicini, dedicated to the contrada from the year 1778.

Contrada of the Snail

In the centre of a silver shield, between the initials U. and M. and the rose buds, there is the symbol of the contrada, a snail. The flag is red and yellow with other inserted devices and bordered by the colour sky-blue. The seat of the contrada is in San Marco Street, close to the Church of Santi Pietro e Paolo, which has been the oratory of the contrada since 1814.

THE SIENA PALIO

On July 2 and on August 16 every year the widely celebrated Palio is held in Siena. It is a festival of medieval origin based on a race of horses ridden bareback, derived from the custom of those ages celebrating the most important festivities with games, often having as a prominent feature the wartime battles and engagements.

The festivities are linked up: the first, with celebration of the «Madonna» (Virgin Mary) of Provenzano, a feast which was begun at the beginning of the 17th century; the second is the oldest, dating back to the 12th century, connected with the celebration of the blessed Virgin Mary. During the centuries the Palio assumed different meanings linked to the political affairs of the town and to its statement of independence. Today the Palio evokes again all the true spirit of the old local pride in a game amongst the numerous town districts («contrade») which, genuinely passionate, contend for the drape. Once the contradas were very numerous, now their number has decreased to 17 and each one of them exists with its own tradition, museum, church and cortège, an intensive year of preparations, training, feasts and rites. Only 10 out of these 17 contradas dispute the game (they are chosen by a standard of turns).

The field of the race is the square of the Campo: it is placed on a ring of earth along the exterior perimeter of the brick-floor and then the trib-

Contrada captain of the Wave

The symbol of this is a crowned dolphin, symbolically swimming into a white and blue sea. The latter have also been the colours of the contrada since 1714, whereas prior to this they were white and black. The seat is in Giovanni Duprè Street, in the surroundings of the San Giuseppe arch. In 1787 the Grand Duke Pietro Leopoldo assigned to the contrada the 16th century Church of San Giuseppe.

Contrada of the Panther

The crowned rampant panther is the symbol of the contrada, inserted, together with a letter U, in red and silver shields. The colours of the contrada are red, sky-blue with some white stripes. The seat is in San Quirico Street and so is the Santi Quirino e Giuditta Church, dedicated to the contrada since 1957.

unes and the jury-box are built around the square. The whole town is covered with flags and standards. On the morning of the game a Holy Mass is celebrated in the Chapel of the Square, while in the cathedral, on August 16, or in the Church of Santa Maria di Provenzano, on July 2, the standards of the «contradas» are hung together, with the Palio intended for the winner. In the afternoon in the contrada churches the horses are blessed. Then the picturesque cortège begins: the multicoloured historical costumes strike the eye in the same way as the flag wavers exercising their skill. The Palio (drape) parades are carried on the «Carroccio» (a carriage bearing the standards of Siena) hauled by some oxes.

The horses, aligned along a long and thick rope, the «Canapo», spring forward when this rope is released running three laps of the square, in a dangerous, violent and wild race. The end of the Palio sees the desperation of the losers and the unbridled joy of the winners and their allies, celebrating throughout the whole night.

The contradas, gathered in thirds, have their own symbols, and flag colours.

Contrada of the Wood

The symbol is a rhino at the foot of a green oak: in the shield there is also a sun on a sky-blue field and the initial U. The colours are green, orange with some white stripes. Since 1818 the contrada oratory and the seat have been in the small San Sebastiano Square.

Contrada of the Turtle

A turtle on a golden field surrounded with knots and alternate daisies is the contrada device. The seat and the museum are in Tommaso Pendola Street, close to the Oratory of Sant'Antonio da Padova erected by the contrada itself in 1684. The colours of the flag are yellow and sky-blue.

THIRD OF SAN MARTINO

Contrada prioress of the Owl

The symbol of the contrada is a crowned owl, roosting on a small branch: on the two sides are impressed the initials U. and M. The colours characterizing the contrada flag are black and red. The seat is in Cecco Angiolieri Street and nearby in the yard of the Castellare degli Ugurgieri the contrada built its own oratory in 1935.

Contrada of the Unicorn

The symbol of this contrada is a rampant unicorn in a shield bordered by sky-blue. On the edge of the shield is visible the writing «Humberti Regis Gratia». On the sky-blue-edged flag are the colours orange and white. The seat of the contrada is in Pantaneto Street, while the oratory has been recently moved to the San Giovannino Church, in the nearby small San Giovanni Battista Pantaneto Square.

Noble contrada of the Conch

The contrada bears as a symbol a silver, crowned shell placed above two coral branches and a knot interlaced with two cyprus roses: all are placed on a sky-blue field. The flag is completely sky-blue too, bordered by yellow and red. In 1680 the contrada inhabitants erected their own oratory in Pispini Street, where now there is also their seat.

Contrada of Valdimontone

This contrada is also called «of the ram», bearing as a symbol a rampant crowned ram having close-by the initial U. The flag is divided into yellow fields and red and white edged fields. Since 1741 the Romanesque Church of San Leonardo is dedicated to the contrada which uses it as an oratory in the Valdimontone Street, where we also find the seat.

Contrada of the Tower

An elephant carrying a tower appears on the contrada shield: in 1887 a red saddlecloth with a white cross and a saddle were added to the symbol. The contrada flag is completely red, adorned with white and blue arabesques. The seat and the old San Giacomo Oratory belonging to the contrada are in Salicotto Street.

Noble contrada of the Caterpillar

The symbol of this contrada is composed of a crowned caterpillar over a branch, and, in the upper part, there is the Savoyard cross. The flag is irregularly divided into yellow and green and is bordered by light- blue. The seat, the museum and the SS. Nome di Dio Oratory, built by the contrada inhabitants in 1680, are in Comune Street.

Contrada of the Dragon

The symbol is a winged crowned dragon sustaining a flag with the initial U. The standard is subdivided into red and green fields with yellow borders. The Santa Caterina Church was assigned to the contrada since 1787; the seat of the contrada, like the church, is in Matteotti Square, ex Poggio Malavolti.

Imperial contrada of the Giraffe

In the contrada shield we can see a giraffe held still with a rope by a Moor and surmounted with a ribbon on which is written «Humbertus I dedit». The contrada flag is white and red. Its seat is in Vergine Street, the oratory has been established below the Collegiata di Santa Maria di Provenzano.

Contrada of the Hedgehog

The symbol of the contrada is a crowned hedgehog, surrounded by roses and by a Savoyard knot, all on a silver field. The flag is completely white with black, red and light-blue arabesques. The seat is in Camollia Street and so is the San Bartolomeo Oratory, in the old Santi Vincenzo e Anastasia Church, dedicated to the contrada since 1788.

Contrada of the She-Wolf

The emblem is composed of a shield bearing a she-wolf suckling the twins and of the Siena white streak. The edge of the shield is white and red with red and white crosses. The colours of the flag are white and black and it is bordered with yellow. In the old San Rocco Church, conceded in 1786, in Vallerozzi Street, there is the oratory and the seat of the contrada.

Noble contrada of the Goose

The symbol of this contrada is a crowned white goose, with a light-blue ribbon around the neck to which is tied the Savoyard cross. The flag is white and green and is red-edged. In 1465 the contrada erected its own seat and the oratory in the surroundings of the Santa Caterina in Fontebranda Sanctuary.

OUTSKIRTS OF SIENA

The rich blend of historical treasures and environments makes this area one of the most impressive and picturesque in Tuscany. Churches, towers, monuments, villages and farms, spread over gentle hills and pleasant valleys, are items of environmental and historical interest.

BASILICA OF THE OBSERVANCE

The Basilica dell'Osservanza is acknowledged to be the most important spot on the outskirts of Siena. It is about two kilometers north of the town, out of the Ovile Gate, on the Chiantigiana Road.

The church, re-built in a similar manner to the original after a disastrous bomb-blast in 1944, dates back to 1474-1490 and scholars have not yet ascribed it to any architect: perhaps it was designed by Giacomo Cozzarelli or Francesco di Giorgio Martini.

In the surroundings there used to be a hermitage built in the 12th century, which in 1404 became that of San Bernardino, and a 15th century church.

The set of volumes is very simple, the façade is preceded by a portico and the dome is inside a cylindrical tiburio. All the elements are made of bricks.

The interior is composed of a single nave dividing eight chapels: the stucco and terracotta medallions of the vault and the chapel are reconstructions derived from the original works of Giacomo Cozzarelli and, the counter-façade, works of Andrea della Robbia. In the interior there are: a triptych by Sano di Pietro, Virgin Mary with the Child between San Girolamo and San Bernardino; a reliquary of San Bernardino by Francesco D'Antonio (1454); a triptych of the Virgin Mary between the Saints Ambrogio and Girolamo (1436), ascribed today to a disciple of Sassetta; a polyptych by Andrea di Bartolo (1413); The Saints Giovanni Battista, Francesco, Pietro and Giovanni Evangelista; Coronation of the Virgin Mary, enamelled terracotta by Andrea della Robbia; a Crucifixion and Saints attributed to Riccio; a Virgin Mary with the Child by Sano di Pietro. The terracottas with figures of Virgin Mary and Archangel Gabriel placed on the triumphal arch are also by Andrea della Robbia.

The works preserved in the Aurelio Castelli Museum are also very interesting: the Crypt, the Loggia of Pandolfo and, lastly, the reconstruction of San Bernardino's cell.

THE CHARTREUSE OF PONTIGNANO

Going out of the Ovile Gate, after about eight kilometers we find the Chartreuse of Pontignano. Built in 1343, it is actually the seat of the Mario Bracci University College. Three cloisters compose the fundamental nucleus: the first, having a well in the middle, is Renaissance

Castle of the Four Towers.

Castle of Belcaro.

style; the second, to which you get through a portal of the 15th century, is a work in bricks of the 15th century, having small stone pillars surmounted with a loggia. From here we enter the third cloister in which are preserved the remains of frescoes by Bernardino Poccetti, the same author of the frescoes inside the church, built by Stefano Cassiani, Orazio Porta and Domenico Brugieri. The wooden choir is a 16th century work by Domenico Atticciati.

THE FOUR TOWERS CASTLE

Another extremely impressive place to visit, in regard to the natural scenery, is the Four Towers Castle. Going out of the town from Gate Pispini and reaching the Arbia valley we can admire the sharp and severe structure of the castle which dates back to the 14th century; built on a quadrilateral plan with towers on the corners it has a well preserved and attractive courtyard.

Not far from the castle there is the Church of Santa Regina, Romanesque architecture of the 12th century, in which there are ample remains of frescoes belonging to the Sienese School of the 15th century.

BELCARO CASTLE

Going out of the town (San Marco Gate) in the direction of Grosseto we turn towards the fascinating Belcaro Castle. It is surrounded by a blooming park and was built in the 12th century, enlarged and then turned into a villa by Baldassarre Peruzzi who built the palace, the loggia and the chapel. In this castle we find Peruzzi's frescoes of the 1536. Giuseppe Pertini completed the transformation in 1868.

LECCETO

A few kilometers away from the Belcaro castle we can admire the Lecceto Augustinian hermitage; it is surrounded by woods, and scholars date it back to the 4th century. The construction still has the typical shape of a fortress-hermitage surmounted with a stone tower. The hermitage is composed of the church, rebuilt in 1317; the portico with monochrome frescoes of the first half of the 15th century; two cloisters, one of the 13th and the other of the 15th century, having a central well, and on the walls, the remains of frescoes.

Augustinian Hermitage of Lecceto.

SAN LEONARDO AT THE LAKE

The Church of San Leonardo al Lago, not far from the Lecceto hermitage, still maintains its 14th century shape, but was a part of an Augustinian hermitage two centuries older, now mostly lost. The style is Romanesque-Gothic and it has a cabin-shaped façade adorned with a portal and a rose-window while inside there is a single nave covered with a vault. The masterpiece by Lippo Vanni, disciple of Pietro Lorenzetti, a fresco in the apse, is remarkable among the remains of the Sienese School during the 14th century and was painted between 1360 and 1370; the music Angels, the Annunciation, the Presentation of the Virgin Mary at the Temple, and the Virgin's Weddings are episodes of this masterpiece.

The church Crypt kept the mortal remains of the Blessed Soul Agostino Novello, who died in 1309, knight of King Manfredi (now in the Sant'Agostino Church in Siena).

PIEVE DI PONTE ALLO SPINO

Going out of the San Marco Gate, on the road to Grosseto, turn towards Pieve di Ponte allo Spino. This beautiful Romanesque construction is characterized by a simple cabin-shaped stone façade with a portal and a window with bas-reliefs, an interesting apse and a bell-tower with simple and mullioned windows. Inside there are three aisles, with old capitals on the pillars, semi-circular apses which are covered with trusses. Outside there is the former monastery, with the remains of the cloister and a beautiful building mullioned windows.

BROLIO CASTLE

On the road to Montevarchi, about 20 kilometers from Siena we find the old (9th century) Brolio Castle which has belonged, since 1141, to the Ricasoli Family. For its strategical value, placed as it was on a ridge of the Chianti Hills, it passed through the domination of Florence, Siena and Aragon. Damaged by a fire, it was freely re-built by Ricasoli from the beginning of 1860. Also of interest is the San Jacopo Chapel (1348), the old forecastle of the manorhouse with towers, the walk of the patrol, and the huge walls. Inside the Noblemen Building we find, in the dining room, old Flemish pieces of tapestry and armours. Not far away there are the edifices in which is produced the vintage wine Brolio.

GENERAL INDEX

Introduction .... p. 2
Tour of the Town no. 1 .... » 10
Tour of the Town no. 2 .... » 25
Tour of the Town no. 3 .... » 60
Tour of the Town no. 4 .... » 84
The Siena Palio .... » 106
Outskirts of Siena .... » 116
Back page: Map of the city

Alphabetic Index

Academy, Chigi Music, 26
Academy of the Intronati, 93
Academy of the Rozzi, 93
Arch of the Two Doors (delle due Porte), 74
Arch of St. Augustine (Sant'Agostino), 76
Arch of St. Francis (San Francesco), 87
Arch of St. Joseph (San Giuseppe), 79
Archbrotherhood of Mercy (della Misericordia), 83
Archives of State, 84

Baptistery, 53
Basilica of San Domenico (St. Dominic), 98
Basilica of St. Francis (San Francesco), 87

Cathedral, 28
Cemetery of Mercy (della Misericordia), 78
Chapel of the Prison of Sant'Ansano, 76
Chapel of the Square, 13
Court of the Castellare degli Ugurgieri, 86
Courtyard of Podestà, 22
Crypt, 52
Churches:
  Company of San Sebastiano, 103
  Refugio (Refuge), 82
  San Bartolomeo (Bartholomew), 103
  San Cristoforo (Christopher), 93
  San Donato, 91
  San Gaetano, 83
  San Giorgio (George), 83
  San Girolamo (Jerome), 79
  San Giovanni Battista della Scala (John the Baptist of the Stairs), 86
  San Giuseppe (Joseph), 78
  San Martino (Martin), 83
  San Niccolò (Nicholas) al Carmine, 75
  San Pellegrino alla Sapienza, 102
  San Pietro (Peter) alla Magione, 104
  San Pietro Ovile, 87
  San Pietro alle Scale, 73
  San Rocco, 91
  San Sebastiano in Valle Piatta, 55
  Santa Caterina (Catherine) in Fonte Branda, 97
  Santa Maria degli Angeli, 82
  Santa Maria di Provenzano, 86
  Santa Maria della Scala (of the Stair), 58
  Santa Maria dei Servi, 80
  Santa Mustiola della Rosa, 78
  Santi Pietro e Paolo (Peter and Paul), 76
  Santi Quirico e Giuditta (Judith), 76
  Sant'Agostino (Augustine), 76
  Sant'Andrea (Andrew), 102
  Santo Spirito, 82
  Santuccio, 82
Fountains:
  Fonte Branda, 94
  Fonte Gaia, (Happy), 11
  Fonte Giusta, (Just), 103
  Fonte Nuova, (New), 91
  Fonte Ovile, 91
  Fonte Pantaneto, 86
  Fort of Santa Barbara, 105
Gates (Porte):
  Camollia, 102
  Ovile, 91
  Pispini, 83
  Romana, 82
  Tufi, 78
Hospital of Santa Maria della Scala, 58
House of the Forteguerri, 27
House of Pia, 73
Interior of Palazzo Pubblico (Public Building), 13
Lizza Park, 105
Logge (Arcades):
  Logge del Papa, 86
  Loggia dell'Indipendenza (of the Independence), 93
  Loggia delle Mercanzie (of the Merchants), 10
Monastery of Santa Marta, 76
Municipal Library of the Intronati, 101
Museums:
  Civic Museum, 14
  Museum of the Metropolitan Institution, 46
  National Archeological Museum, 105
National Picture Gallery (Pinacoteca Nazionale), 60
New Cathedral, 46
Oratories:
  della Madonna del Rosario (of the Rosary), 76
  di San Bernardino, 90

di San Giacomo, 79
di Santa Maria delle Nevi (of the Snows), 92
della Santissima Trinità (of the Holy Trinity), 81
Palaces (Palazzi) and Public Buildings:
Archbishop's Palace, 59
Ballati, 93
Bichi-Ruspoli, 93
Buonsignori, 60
Capitano, 28
Chigi alla Postierla, 28
Chigi-Saracini, 25
Chigi-Zondadari, 24
Cinughi, 83
Costantini, 102
Elci, 24
Gori-Pannilini, 93
Marsili, 27
Palmieri-Nuti, 93
Patrizi, 25
Piccolomini, 84
Piccolomini delle Papesse (of the Female Popes), 26
Pollini, 75
Pubblico, 11
Salimbeni, 92
San Galgano, 82
Sansedoni, 24
Spannocchi, 92
Tolomei, 93
Sanctuary of Santa Caterina, 94
Squares (Piazze):
Campo (of the Field), 10
Duomo (of the Cathedral), 28
Indipendenza (of the Independence), 93
Mercato (of the Market), 79
Postierla, 27
Salimbeni, 92
Tolomei, 93
Theatre of the Rozzi, 93
Tower of Mangia, 11
Tower of Rocchetta, 76
University, 86
Via Pier Andrea Mattioli, 78
Via Roma, 82
Via Stalloreggi, 74

Legend:

1. Piazza del Campo (Square of the Field)
2. National Picture Gallery - *Via S. Pietro 29*
3. Church of S. Pietro alle Scale - *Via S. Pietro*
4. Prato S. Agostino - *corner Via S. Agata - Via A. Mattioli*
5. Cathedral - Museum of the Metropolitan Institution - crypt - Baptistery - *Piazza Duomo*
6. Piazza del Mercato (Market square)
7. Church of Santa Maria dei Servi - *Piazza A. Manzoni*
8. Church of S. Spirito - *Piazza S. Santo Spirito*
9. Church of S. Giorgio - *Via Banchi di Sotto*
10. Church of S. Martino - *Via Banchi di Sotto*
11. Logge del Papa - *Via Banchi di Sotto*
12. Piccolomini Palace - *Via Banchi di Sotto*
13. Church of S. Maria di Provenzano - *Piazza Provenzano*
14. Basilica of S. Francesco - *Piazza S. Francesco*
15. Ex-convent of S. Francesco - *Piazza S. Francesco*
16. Church of S. Donato - *Piazza Abbadia*
17. Salimbeni Palace - *Piazza Salimbeni*
18. Tolomei Palace - *Via Banchi di Sopra*
19. Church of S. Cristoforo - *Piazza Tolomei*
20. Branda Fountain - *Via Fonte Branda*
21. Sanctuary of S. Caterina - *Via del Tiratoio 15*
22. Church of S. Giuseppe - *Via S. Agata*
23. Basilica of S. Domenico - *Piazza S. Domenico*
24. Church of S. Niccolò al Carmine - *Piano dei Mantellini*
25. Hospital of S. Maria della Scala and the National Archeological Museum (being transferred) - *Piazza Duomo*

Graphics and Pagination: Federico Frassinetti
Photography: Ascanio Ascani Misano (Fo)
Foto Studio Gielle, Siena - Federico Frassinetti, Bologna
Foto Barone, Firenze

Translations: Art, Bologna

publisher: **ITALCARDS** Bologna - Italy

Printed at LA FOTOMETALGRAFICA EMILIANA
San Lazzaro di Savena, Bologna